GREAT LIVES

MARIE
CURIE

D0063782

First edition for the United States, Canada, and the Philippines published in 2019 by B.E.S. Publishing

All inquiries should be addressed to:
B.E.S. Publishing
250 Wireless Boulevard
Hauppauge, NY 11788
www.bes-publishing.com

ISBN: 978-1-4380-1204-9

Library of Congress Control No.: 2018963805

Conceived, designed, and produced by The Bright Press,
an imprint of The Quarto Group.
The Old Brewery, 6 Blundell Street,
London, N7 9BH, United Kingdom
T (0) 20 7700 6700 F (0) 20 7700 8066
www.QuartoKnows.com

Publisher: Mark Searle
Creative Director: James Evans
Managing Editor: Jacqui Sayers
Editor: Judith Chamberlain
Project Editors: Anna Southgate, Lucy York
Art Director: Katherine Radcliffe
Design: Lyndsey Harwood and Geoff Borin

Date of Manufacture: March 2019
Manufactured by: Hung Hing Printing, Shenzhen, China

Printed in China

9 8 7 6 5 4 3 2 1

GREAT LIVES
MARIE CURIE

By Agnieszka Biskup
with illustrations by Sonia Leong

PUBLISHING

CONTENTS

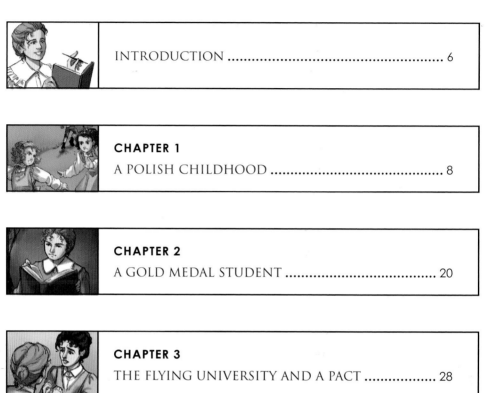

INTRODUCTION

When Maria Skłodowska was born, in 1867, to two Polish schoolteachers, no one could have realized the profound effect that her discoveries were to have upon the world. Maria, known as Madame Marie Curie after she married French physicist Pierre Curie, was a trailblazer, both as a scientist and as a woman.

Marie was the first woman ever to obtain a doctorate of science degree in Europe, the first woman to win the prestigious Nobel Prize, the first woman to lecture at the Sorbonne University in Paris, and the first person—man or woman—to win two Nobel Prizes. She discovered two new elements (polonium and radium), coined the word radioactivity, and figured out that the ability to emit radiation was linked to the interior of the atom. With this revolutionary insight, she helped usher in the atomic age, paving the way for other scientists to investigate subatomic particles.

Though Marie didn't really care for publicity or honors, she nonetheless became one of the most famous people in the world. She found it endlessly fascinating why the public would be interested in her life, rather than her scientific work. She would tell reporters: "In science we must be interested in things, not in persons."

Whether Marie thought so or not, her personal life was very interesting, too. Romantic and tragic by turns, it involved illness,

scandals, love affairs, duels, gossip, and newspaper headlines, as well as great honors and harsh disappointments. Through it all, however, ran Marie's determination to learn and discover all she could. She was a passionate Polish patriot during a time in which Poland wasn't an independent country. Educational opportunities for Poles and women were limited, so Marie studied illegally at secret underground schools. She could have been arrested if discovered.

Marie was so determined to obtain a university education that she worked as a governess for several years to save money to study in France. This was at a time when most women were not encouraged to study at all. Instead of concentrating on church, children, and the kitchen, Marie wanted to live in a world of pure knowledge and selfless research and discovery. She encountered multiple barriers and prejudices in her quest, not only because she was a woman, but also because she was a foreigner in a strange land. She was lucky to meet Pierre Curie, her future husband, a brilliant physicist in his own right and as passionate about science as she was. Unlike most men of his time, he encouraged Marie in her work and dropped his own research to work on hers once he realized how important it was to the world.

The radioactive elements polonium and radium made the Curies famous, but also harmed their health. Marie and Pierre were exposed to dangerous amounts of radiation and suffered for it. Even now, Marie's clothes and notebooks will remain radioactive for 1,600 years. Interestingly, her notebooks are stored in lead-lined boxes.

Today, Marie Curie remains a great source of inspiration to many. Read on to discover how she did it.

CHAPTER 1

A POLISH CHILDHOOD

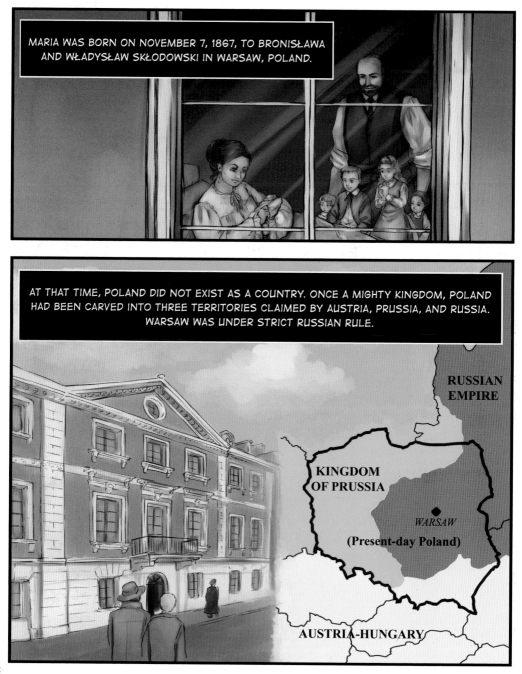

MARIA WAS BORN ON NOVEMBER 7, 1867, TO BRONISŁAWA AND WŁADYSŁAW SKŁODOWSKI IN WARSAW, POLAND.

AT THAT TIME, POLAND DID NOT EXIST AS A COUNTRY. ONCE A MIGHTY KINGDOM, POLAND HAD BEEN CARVED INTO THREE TERRITORIES CLAIMED BY AUSTRIA, PRUSSIA, AND RUSSIA. WARSAW WAS UNDER STRICT RUSSIAN RULE.

RUSSIAN EMPIRE

KINGDOM OF PRUSSIA

WARSAW

(Present-day Poland)

AUSTRIA-HUNGARY

THE POLES FOUGHT TO REGAIN THEIR HOMELAND SEVERAL TIMES. IN 1863, JUST A FEW YEARS BEFORE MARIA'S BIRTH, THOUSANDS OF POLES (INCLUDING MEMBERS OF BRONISŁAWA AND WŁADYSŁAW'S FAMILIES) ROSE UP AGAINST THEIR RUSSIAN RULERS IN WHAT WAS CALLED THE JANUARY UPRISING.

BUT, AS IN THE PAST, THIS UPRISING FAILED. THE POLES, FIGHTING WITH SCYTHES AND CLUBS, WERE NO MATCH FOR THE NUMEROUS, WELL-ARMED RUSSIAN TROOPS. POLES WHO FOUGHT WERE BANISHED TO THE FROZEN WASTELANDS OF SIBERIA IN NORTHERN RUSSIA...

...AND THEIR LEADERS WERE PUBLICLY EXECUTED.

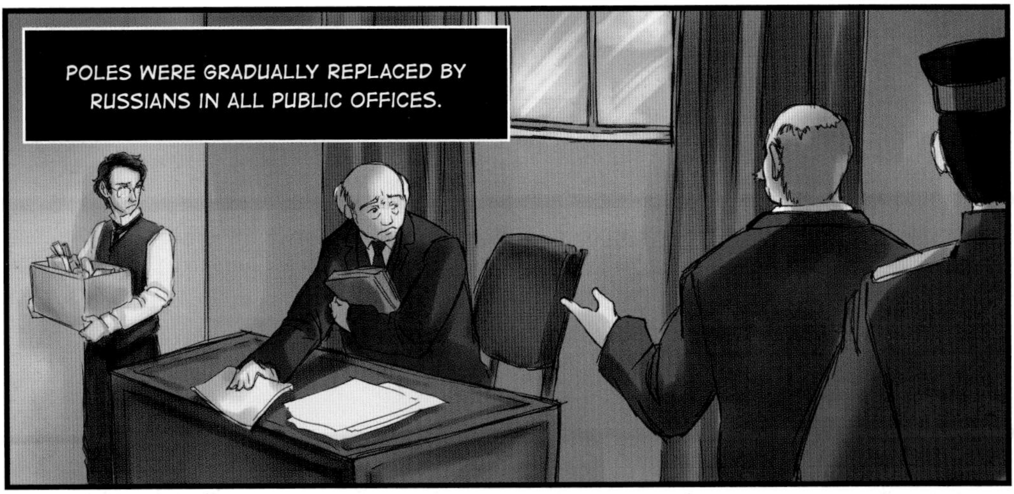
POLES WERE GRADUALLY REPLACED BY RUSSIANS IN ALL PUBLIC OFFICES.

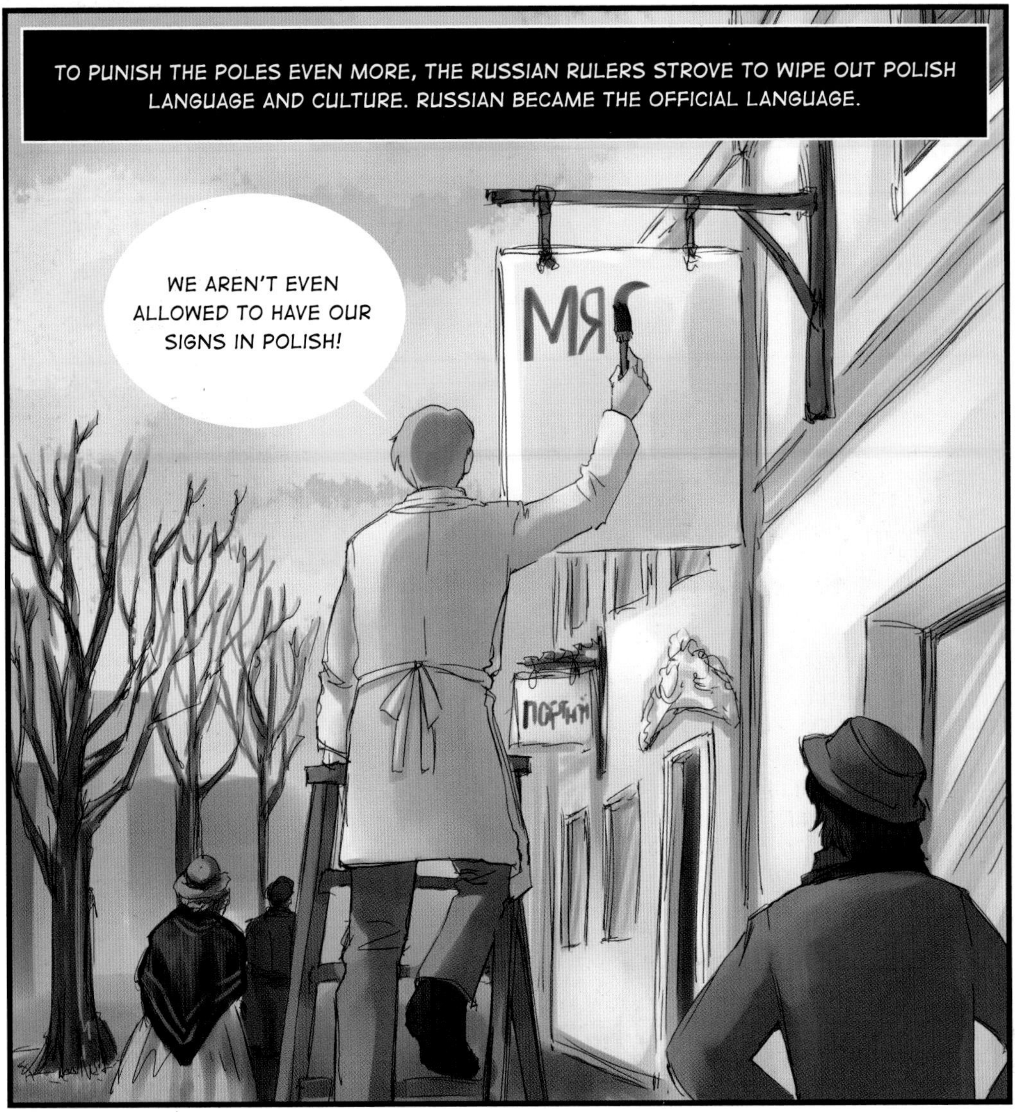
TO PUNISH THE POLES EVEN MORE, THE RUSSIAN RULERS STROVE TO WIPE OUT POLISH LANGUAGE AND CULTURE. RUSSIAN BECAME THE OFFICIAL LANGUAGE.
WE AREN'T EVEN ALLOWED TO HAVE OUR SIGNS IN POLISH!
МЯС

SPIES WERE EVERYWHERE, READY TO REPORT ANY VIOLATIONS.

WE COULD LOSE OUR JOBS OR BE SENT AWAY TO SIBERIA IF THEY HEAR US SAY ANYTHING AGAINST THE RUSSIANS!

ALL CLASSES IN STATE-APPROVED SCHOOLS WERE TO BE TAUGHT IN RUSSIAN FROM RUSSIAN BOOKS. YOU COULD GET A DIPLOMA ONLY FROM ONE OF THESE SCHOOLS.

LET US STUDY OUR RUSSIAN HISTORY.

WHEN MARIA WAS OLDER, SHE WROTE ABOUT WHAT IT WAS LIKE TO LIVE AS A CHILD UNDER RUSSIAN RULE:

"CONSTANTLY HELD IN SUSPICION AND SPIED UPON, THE CHILDREN KNEW THAT A SINGLE CONVERSATION IN POLISH, OR AN IMPRUDENT WORD, MIGHT SERIOUSLY HARM, NOT ONLY THEMSELVES, BUT THEIR FAMILIES."

DESPITE THE RUSSIAN OCCUPATION, MARIA'S EARLY CHILDHOOD WAS HAPPY.

WŁADYSŁAW, HER FATHER, TAUGHT MATH AND PHYSICS AT A BOYS' SCHOOL.

BRONISŁAWA, HER MOTHER, WAS UNUSUALLY WELL-EDUCATED FOR A WOMAN OF THE TIME. SHE WAS THE PRINCIPAL OF A PRESTIGIOUS GIRLS' SCHOOL.

THEY PASSED ON THEIR LOVE OF LEARNING (AND POLAND) TO THEIR FIVE CHILDREN: ZOFIA, JÓZEF, BRONIA, HELENA, AND ESPECIALLY, MARIA, THE YOUNGEST. HER PARENTS TAUGHT ALL FIVE CHILDREN A WIDE RANGE OF SUBJECTS AND SKILLS.

CHILDREN, HERE'S A NEW HISTORY BOOK FOR US TO READ!

IN THE SKŁODOWSKI HOUSEHOLD, LEARNING WAS PLAY. THEIR FATHER TURNED EVERY CONVERSATION INTO A LESSON. HE CREATED GAMES TO TEACH THE CHILDREN GEOGRAPHY AND GAVE THEM MATH PROBLEMS TO SOLVE FOR FUN.

LET'S USE THE GREEN BLOCKS FOR CONTINENTS AND THE BLUE ONES FOR RIVERS!

ON SATURDAY EVENINGS, HE WOULD READ ALOUD TO THE CHILDREN FROM FORBIDDEN POLISH WORKS, INCLUDING POETRY.

TONIGHT WE START *PAN TADEUSZ* BY OUR GREAT POET ADAM MICKIEWICZ.

WHEN SHE WAS VERY LITTLE, MARIA WAS FASCINATED BY HER FATHER'S SCIENTIFIC EQUIPMENT.

WHAT IS THAT, PAPA?

IT'S MY EQUIPMENT FOR MY SCIENCE CLASSES—MY PHYSICS APPARATUS.

WHAT A FUNNY NAME!

PHY-SICS APP-A-RA-TUS.

THE SKŁODOWSKIS SPENT THEIR SUMMERS WITH RELATIVES IN THE POLISH COUNTRYSIDE. THE CHILDREN LOVED PLAYING IN THE FIELDS AND WOODS.

COME CATCH ME, BRONIA!

BUT EVEN IN THE COUNTRY, THERE WAS STILL TIME TO LEARN. BRONIA, WHO WAS SEVEN, WAS LEARNING TO READ. SHE USED CARDBOARD CARDS WITH LETTERS ON THEM THAT MARIA, AGE FOUR, SHUFFLED FOR HER.

GIVE ME ANOTHER CARD, MARIA.

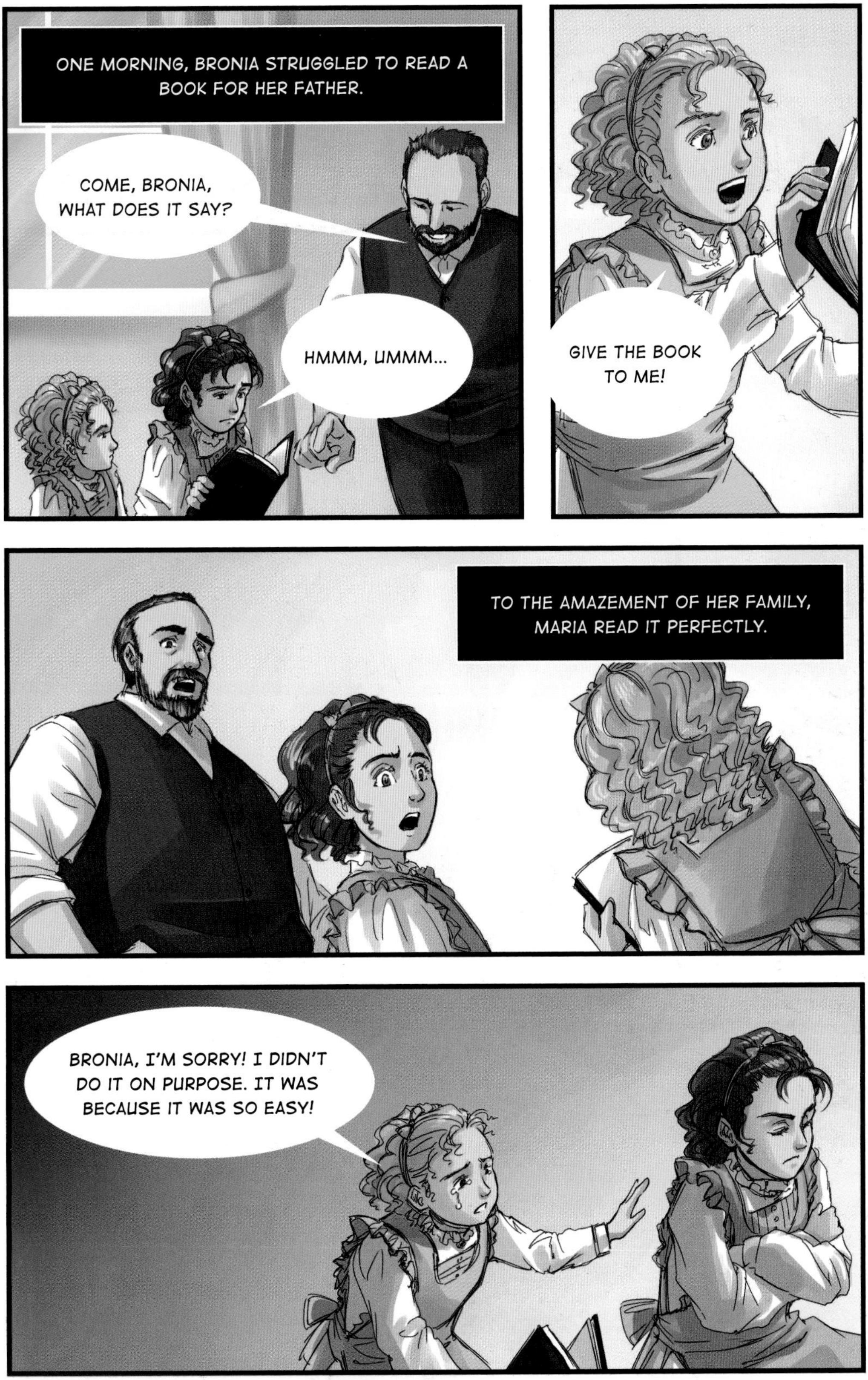
ONE MORNING, BRONIA STRUGGLED TO READ A BOOK FOR HER FATHER.
COME, BRONIA, WHAT DOES IT SAY?
HMMM, UMMM...
GIVE THE BOOK TO ME!
TO THE AMAZEMENT OF HER FAMILY, MARIA READ IT PERFECTLY.
BRONIA, I'M SORRY! I DIDN'T DO IT ON PURPOSE. IT WAS BECAUSE IT WAS SO EASY!

BUT A SHADOW HUNG OVER THE FAMILY. THEIR MOTHER SUFFERED FROM TUBERCULOSIS. AT THAT TIME, THERE WAS NO REAL TREATMENT OR CURE FOR THE DISEASE. SHE TRIED TO AVOID KISSING AND TOUCHING HER CHILDREN SO THEY WOULDN'T GET SICK.

STAY AWAY, CHILDREN!

EVENTUALLY SHE STOPPED TEACHING AND WOULD SPEND LONG PERIODS AWAY FROM WARSAW IN SPECIAL HOSPITALS TRYING TO GET BETTER. ZOFIA, THE ELDEST, WOULD GO WITH HER TO HELP TAKE CARE OF HER.

PAPA, WHY DOES MAMA HAVE TO LEAVE?

WE NEED MAMA TO HAVE FRESH AIR AND REST SO SHE CAN GET BETTER.

IN 1873, MORE MISFORTUNES STRUCK THE FAMILY. THEIR FATHER'S POSITION AND SALARY WERE REDUCED AT HIS SCHOOL. HE LOST HIS SAVINGS IN A BAD INVESTMENT. WITH THE ADDITIONAL COSTS OF THEIR MOTHER'S TREATMENTS, THE FAMILY FELL ON HARD TIMES.

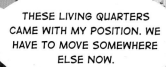

THESE LIVING QUARTERS CAME WITH MY POSITION. WE HAVE TO MOVE SOMEWHERE ELSE NOW.

TO HELP MAKE ENDS MEET, THE SKŁODOWSKIS TURNED THEIR NEW HOME INTO A BOARDING SCHOOL. THE STUDENTS WOULD EAT, SLEEP, AND BE TUTORED IN THESE CRAMPED QUARTERS. THE HOUSE WAS EXTREMELY CROWDED AND OFTEN NOISY. SOME OF THE BOYS WOULD STUDY QUIETLY, BUT OTHERS WOULD ARGUE AND EVEN FIGHT.

HEY, JÓZEF, DO YOU HAVE THE ANSWER TO PROBLEM FIVE?

PIOTR! COME TAKE A LOOK AT THIS!

WHAT ABOUT PROBLEM FOUR?

SHHH! NO YELLING—YOU KNOW PROFESSOR SKŁODOWSKI WANTS US TO KEEP IT DOWN— HIS WIFE IS SICK.

WHO HAS MY LATIN TEXTBOOK?

WITH ALL THE BOARDERS, I HAVE TO SLEEP ON A COUCH IN THE DINING ROOM!

IN 1876, ANOTHER TRAGEDY STRUCK THE SKŁODOWSKIS. POSSIBLY DUE TO THEIR HOUSE BEING SO CROWDED AND GERMS BEING PASSED SO EASILY, BOTH BRONIA AND ZOFIA FELL ILL WITH TYPHUS, A DEADLY INFECTIOUS DISEASE. THEY SHOOK AND MOANED FROM FEVER.

I FEEL SO HOT!

BRONIA RECOVERED, BUT FOURTEEN-YEAR-OLD ZOFIA DID NOT.

HER MOTHER HAD TO BE ALMOST PHYSICALLY FORCED TO STAY HOME (BECAUSE SHE WAS TOO ILL TO GO OUT) ON THE DAY OF HER DAUGHTER'S FUNERAL.

SOB!

MY DARLING ZOFIA! I CAN'T BEAR IT!

ZOFIA'S DEATH CRUSHED THEIR MOTHER. ANOTHER REST CURE WAS ATTEMPTED, BUT IT DID NO GOOD. SHE GREW WEAKER AND WEAKER. ON MAY 8, 1878, SHE CALLED HER CHILDREN TO HER BEDSIDE AND MADE THE SIGN OF THE CROSS OVER THEIR HEADS.

I LOVE YOU ALL.

SHE DIED THE NEXT DAY.

MARIA WAS DEVASTATED BY THE LOSS OF HER MOTHER AND SISTER.

CHAPTER 2

A Gold Medal Student

IN HER SADNESS, MARIA LOST HERSELF IN HER STUDIES AND HER BOOKS.

SHE WAS ALWAYS SMART, AND ONE STORY BECAME A PART OF HER FAMILY'S FOLKLORE.

THE PRIVATE SCHOOL MARIA ATTENDED WAS CLOSELY WATCHED BY THE POLICE AND SCHOOL INSPECTORS TO MAKE SURE THE STUDENTS WERE BEING TAUGHT IN THE APPROVED RUSSIAN MANNER. AGAINST THE RULES, THE TEACHER WAS GIVING A SECRET LESSON ON POLISH HISTORY IN POLISH.

GIRLS, OPEN YOUR HISTORY BOOKS TO PAGE—.

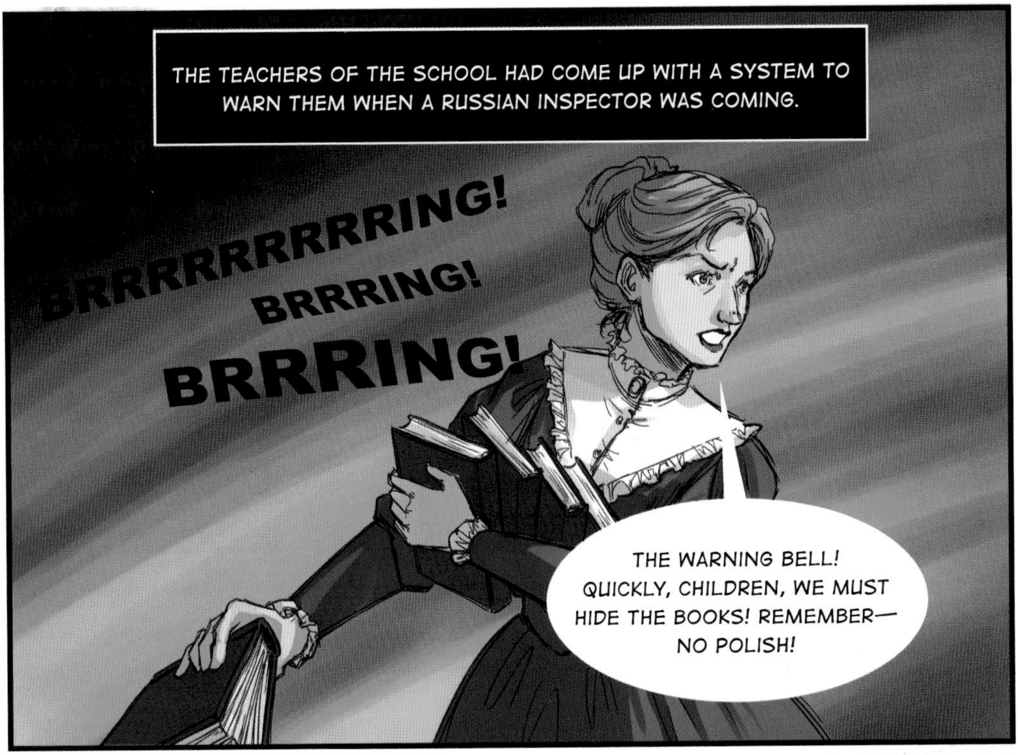
THE TEACHERS OF THE SCHOOL HAD COME UP WITH A SYSTEM TO WARN THEM WHEN A RUSSIAN INSPECTOR WAS COMING.
BRRRRRRRRRING!
BRRRING!
BRRRING!
THE WARNING BELL! QUICKLY, CHILDREN, WE MUST HIDE THE BOOKS! REMEMBER— NO POLISH!

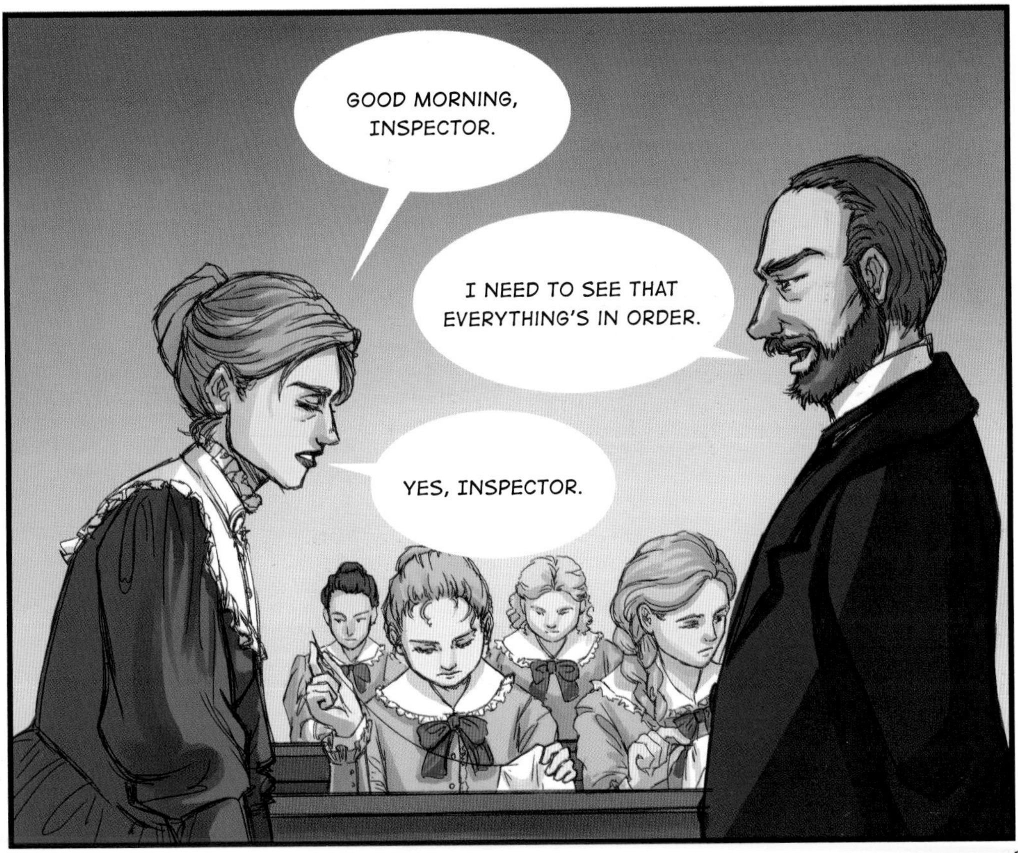
GOOD MORNING, INSPECTOR.
I NEED TO SEE THAT EVERYTHING'S IN ORDER.
YES, INSPECTOR.

WHEN THE INSPECTOR CAME, MARIA WAS ALWAYS CALLED ON BECAUSE SHE WAS THE BEST STUDENT AND HER RUSSIAN WAS PERFECT. BUT SHE HATED BEING QUESTIONED AND IT MADE HER FEEL NERVOUS.

NAME THE TSARS WHO HAVE REIGNED OVER RUSSIA SINCE CATHERINE II...TELL ME THE NAMES AND TITLES OF THE IMPERIAL FAMILY...WHO RULES OVER US?

MARIA ANSWERED ALL THE QUESTIONS CORRECTLY, TURNING WHITER AND WHITER. SHE FELT HUMILIATED.

GOOD, GOOD. UNTIL NEXT TIME—I STILL HAVE OTHER CLASSROOMS TO VISIT TODAY.

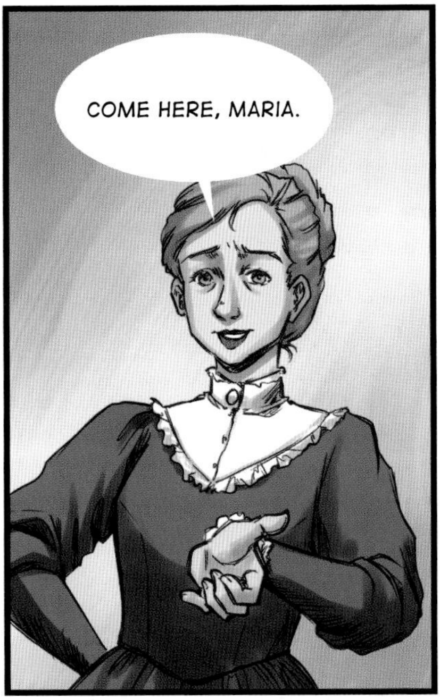
COME HERE, MARIA.

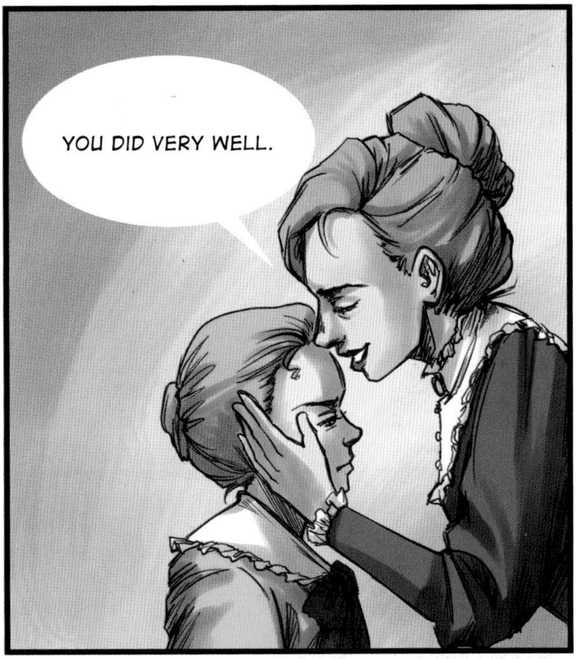
YOU DID VERY WELL.

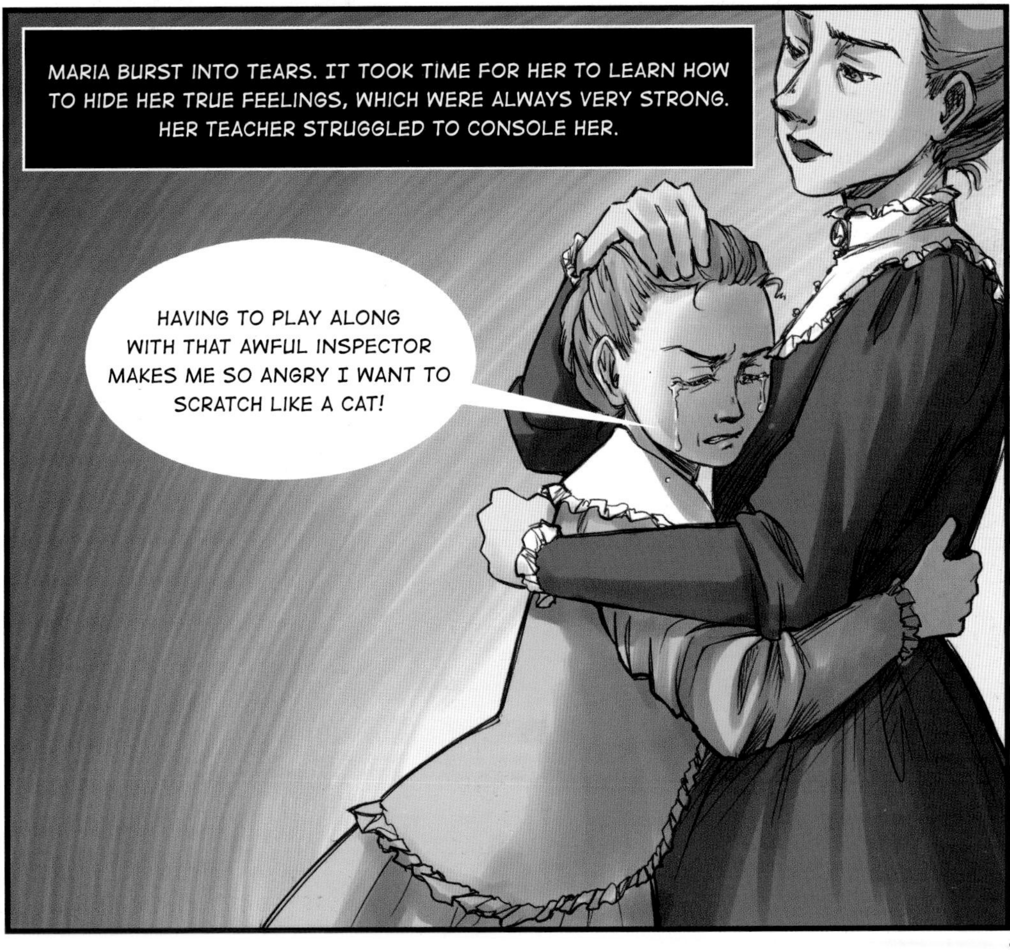
MARIA BURST INTO TEARS. IT TOOK TIME FOR HER TO LEARN HOW TO HIDE HER TRUE FEELINGS, WHICH WERE ALWAYS VERY STRONG. HER TEACHER STRUGGLED TO CONSOLE HER.
HAVING TO PLAY ALONG WITH THAT AWFUL INSPECTOR MAKES ME SO ANGRY I WANT TO SCRATCH LIKE A CAT!

MARIA IS UNDER A LOT OF PRESSURE. I KNOW THAT SHE IS STILL VERY SAD ABOUT HER MOTHER AND SISTER. PERHAPS YOU SHOULD CONSIDER HAVING MARIA TAKE A YEAR OFF FROM HER STUDIES.

I THINK MARIA WOULD DO BETTER IF SHE WENT TO THE RUSSIAN STATE SCHOOL TO EARN HER DIPLOMA. PERHAPS A NEW CHALLENGE WILL HELP KEEP HER MIND OFF HER TROUBLES.

HER OLDER SIBLINGS JÓZEF AND BRONIA HAD ALSO GONE TO THE GOVERNMENT-RUN SECONDARY SCHOOLS. AND NOW IT WAS MARIA'S TURN. SO IN THE FALL OF 1878, MARIA ENROLLED AT THE GIRLS' GYMNASIUM NUMBER 3 IN WARSAW.

IT'S SO BIG—AND SO DIFFERENT FROM MY OTHER SCHOOL.

MARIA WORKED HARDER THAN EVER. MATH AND PHYSICS CAME MOST EASILY TO HER, BUT SHE EXCELLED IN ALL HER CLASSES. SHE MADE FRIENDS, WHICH MADE THE RIGID SCHOOL RULES MORE BEARABLE.

KAZIA, I CAN'T BELIEVE THE TEACHERS WON'T EVEN LET US SPEAK POLISH PRIVATELY! CAN YOU BELIEVE IT? THEY TREAT US LIKE ENEMIES!

I KNOW! I HATE IT, TOO!

BUT IN SPITE OF EVERYTHING—AND YOU CAN MAKE FUN OF ME—I LIKE SCHOOL. I WANT TO LEARN AS MUCH AS I CAN.

IN 1883, MARIA GRADUATED WITH HER DIPLOMA. AT AGE FIFTEEN, SHE WAS YOUNGER THAN ALL THE OTHER GIRLS IN HER CLASS. SHE ALSO WON THE COVETED GOLD MEDAL FOR BEING THE BEST STUDENT.

I EXPECTED NOTHING LESS— MY MARIA WINS THE GOLD MEDAL JUST LIKE JÓZEF AND BRONIA DID BEFORE HER!

MARIA WORKED SO HARD SHE STUDIED HERSELF INTO EXHAUSTION AND COLLAPSE. HER SADNESS RETURNED AND HER FATHER WAS WORRIED ABOUT HER.

MARIA, WHY DON'T YOU VISIT YOUR UNCLES IN THE SOUTH? YOU LIKE BEING IN THE COUNTRY SO MUCH.

GOODBYE, PAPA!

MARIA ENJOYED A FULL YEAR OF FUN AND FREEDOM IN THE COUNTRY.

SHE SLEPT LATE...

...WENT ON SLEIGH RIDES IN THE SNOW AT NIGHT...

...COLLECTED BERRIES...

...WENT ON LONG WALKS...

...READ BOOKS JUST FOR FUN...

...WROTE POEMS...

...DRESSED IN TRADITIONAL POLISH COSTUME...

"DEAR KAZIA, I CAN'T BELIEVE GEOMETRY OR ALGEBRA EVER EXISTED. I HAVE COMPLETELY FORGOTTEN THEM...I DON'T DO A THING...IN SPITE OF MY DIPLOMA...I FEEL INCREDIBLY STUPID. SOMETIMES I LAUGH ALL BY MYSELF, AND I CONTEMPLATE MY STATE OF TOTAL STUPIDITY WITH GENUINE SATISFACTION."

...WENT FISHING...

...SWAM...

...VISITED THE MOUNTAINS....

...WENT TO PARTIES WHERE SHE DANCED POLISH DANCES LIKE THE OBEREK AND THE MAZURKA AND WORE OUT HER DANCING SHOES...

...PLAYED GAMES LIKE TAG AND GOOSE WITH HER COUSINS...

AND NOW BACK HOME TO WARSAW!

...AND SANG POLISH PATRIOTIC SONGS WITHOUT THE WORRY OF GOING TO PRISON.

CHAPTER 3

THE FLYING UNIVERSITY AND A PACT

BY THIS TIME, WŁADYSŁAW HAD STOPPED TAKING IN BOARDING STUDENTS AND HAD MOVED TO A SMALLER APARTMENT.

I WANTED TO SEND YOU ABROAD AND GIVE YOU THE BEST EDUCATION, BUT I BARELY HAVE ENOUGH MONEY FOR MY FOOD AND RENT. WHAT IS TO BECOME OF YOU?

YES PAPA! WE'LL TUTOR TO EARN MONEY.

WE HAVE OUR DIPLOMAS NOW. WE CAN GIVE PRIVATE LESSONS.

LET'S START WITH SOME ARITHMETIC PROBLEMS...

AT THE SAME TIME, MARIA AND BRONIA JOINED A NEW ORGANIZATION WHERE GIRLS SEEKING A HIGHER LEVEL OF EDUCATION WERE SECRETLY TAUGHT IN PRIVATE HOMES ALL OVER WARSAW.

THE CLASSES HAD TO KEEP MOVING FROM PLACE TO PLACE SO THE RUSSIAN POLICE WOULDN'T FIND THEM, HENCE THE NAME "FLYING UNIVERSITY."

IF WE'RE DISCOVERED BY THE POLICE, WE COULD BE SENT TO PRISON.

BUT ISN'T LEARNING WORTH IT? AND WITH WHAT WE'LL LEARN, WE'LL TEACH OTHERS AND HELP POLAND IN THE PROCESS!

I LOVE THE FLYING UNIVERSITY, BUT I WANT TO LEARN MORE. THEY DON'T ACCEPT GIRLS AT WARSAW UNIVERSITY.

I WANT TO BE A DOCTOR, BUT I CAN'T GET MY DEGREE HERE EITHER. THE SORBONNE IN PARIS, FRANCE, ACCEPTS WOMEN STUDENTS. IT'S ONE OF THE BEST UNIVERSITIES IN THE WORLD.

LOOKING AT OUR SAVINGS, WE DON'T MAKE ENOUGH MONEY TUTORING TO STUDY ABROAD.

WHY DON'T I GET A JOB AS A GOVERNESS AND SEND YOU MY WAGES SO YOU CAN STUDY IN PARIS? ONCE YOU'RE A DOCTOR, YOU CAN HELP ME GO TO UNIVERSITY. PAPA SAID HE'D HELP, TOO.

YOU'D BE WILLING TO WAIT UNTIL I'M DONE WITH UNIVERSITY? WHY SHOULD I BE FIRST?

BECAUSE YOU'RE TWENTY AND I'M ONLY SEVENTEEN. I'VE GOT TIME. THIS WILL WORK!

SO YOU SPEAK GERMAN, RUSSIAN, FRENCH, POLISH, AND ENGLISH FLUENTLY?

YES, MADAME, THOUGH MY ENGLISH IS NOT AS GOOD AS THE OTHERS. I ALSO HAVE RECOMMENDATIONS FROM THE PARENTS OF MY PREVIOUS PUPILS.

LET ME SEE WHAT I CAN FIND—I'LL BE IN TOUCH.

IN JANUARY 1886, MARIA OBTAINED A POSITION AS A GOVERNESS TO THE CHILDREN OF JULIUSZ ŻÓRAWSKI, A SUPERVISOR OF A SUGAR BEET FACTORY FAR AWAY FROM WARSAW. (THE PAY WAS BETTER AWAY FROM THE CITY.)

I'M GOING TO BE COMPLETELY ALONE AND INDEPENDENT FOR THE FIRST TIME IN MY LIFE.

AFTER A FOUR-HOUR-LONG SLEIGH RIDE FROM THE TRAIN, MARIA, EXHAUSTED, FINALLY ARRIVED AT THE HOUSE WHERE SHE WOULD WORK FOR THE NEXT THREE YEARS.

WELCOME, WELCOME!

LET ME GET YOU SOME HOT TEA! YOU MUST BE FROZEN AFTER YOUR LONG JOURNEY! AND THEN I'LL SHOW YOU YOUR ROOM.

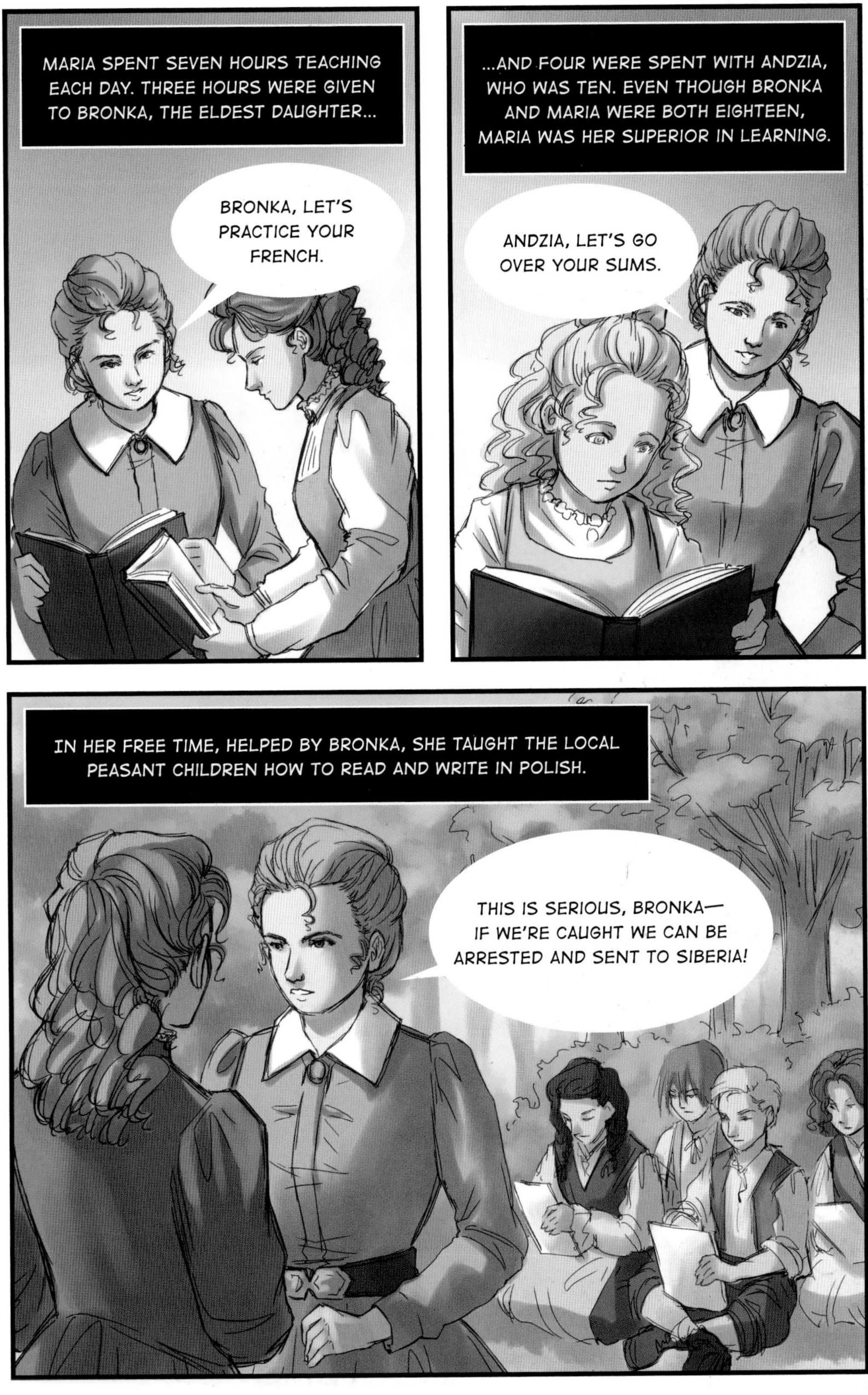
MARIA SPENT SEVEN HOURS TEACHING EACH DAY. THREE HOURS WERE GIVEN TO BRONKA, THE ELDEST DAUGHTER...
BRONKA, LET'S PRACTICE YOUR FRENCH.
...AND FOUR WERE SPENT WITH ANDZIA, WHO WAS TEN. EVEN THOUGH BRONKA AND MARIA WERE BOTH EIGHTEEN, MARIA WAS HER SUPERIOR IN LEARNING.
ANDZIA, LET'S GO OVER YOUR SUMS.
IN HER FREE TIME, HELPED BY BRONKA, SHE TAUGHT THE LOCAL PEASANT CHILDREN HOW TO READ AND WRITE IN POLISH.
THIS IS SERIOUS, BRONKA— IF WE'RE CAUGHT WE CAN BE ARRESTED AND SENT TO SIBERIA!

AT NIGHT, MARIA STUDIED AND READ AND STUDIED SOME MORE.

I'M DETERMINED TO BE PREPARED WHEN IT'S MY TURN TO GO TO UNIVERSITY!

LITTLE BY LITTLE, BY READING AND STUDYING EVERY SUBJECT FROM LITERATURE TO SOCIOLOGY TO ANATOMY, MARIA HONED IN ON WHAT INTERESTED HER MOST.

I NOW KNOW THAT I WANT TO STUDY SCIENCE, ESPECIALLY MATHEMATICS AND PHYSICS. I'M SO GLAD THAT FATHER SENDS ME MATH PROBLEMS TO SOLVE SO I CAN KEEP MY MIND SHARP.

DURING THIS TIME, MARIA MET KAZIMIERZ, THE ELDEST SON OF THE ŻÓRAWSKIS, WHO WAS VISITING ON HIS SCHOOL BREAK FROM WARSAW UNIVERSITY.

YOU MUST BE THE GOVERNESS.

YOU MUST TELL ME ALL THE NEWS OF WARSAW. I HEAR YOU'RE A MATH STUDENT? I'M WORKING ON A PROBLEM THAT I'D LIKE TO DISCUSS WITH YOU...

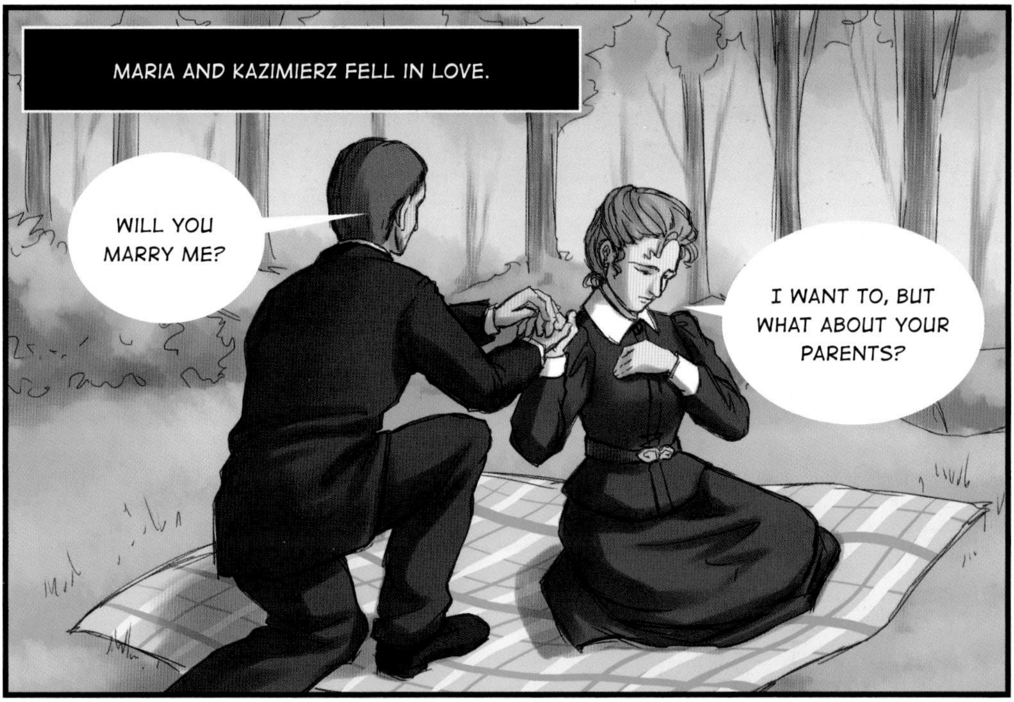
MARIA AND KAZIMIERZ FELL IN LOVE.
WILL YOU MARRY ME?
I WANT TO, BUT WHAT ABOUT YOUR PARENTS?

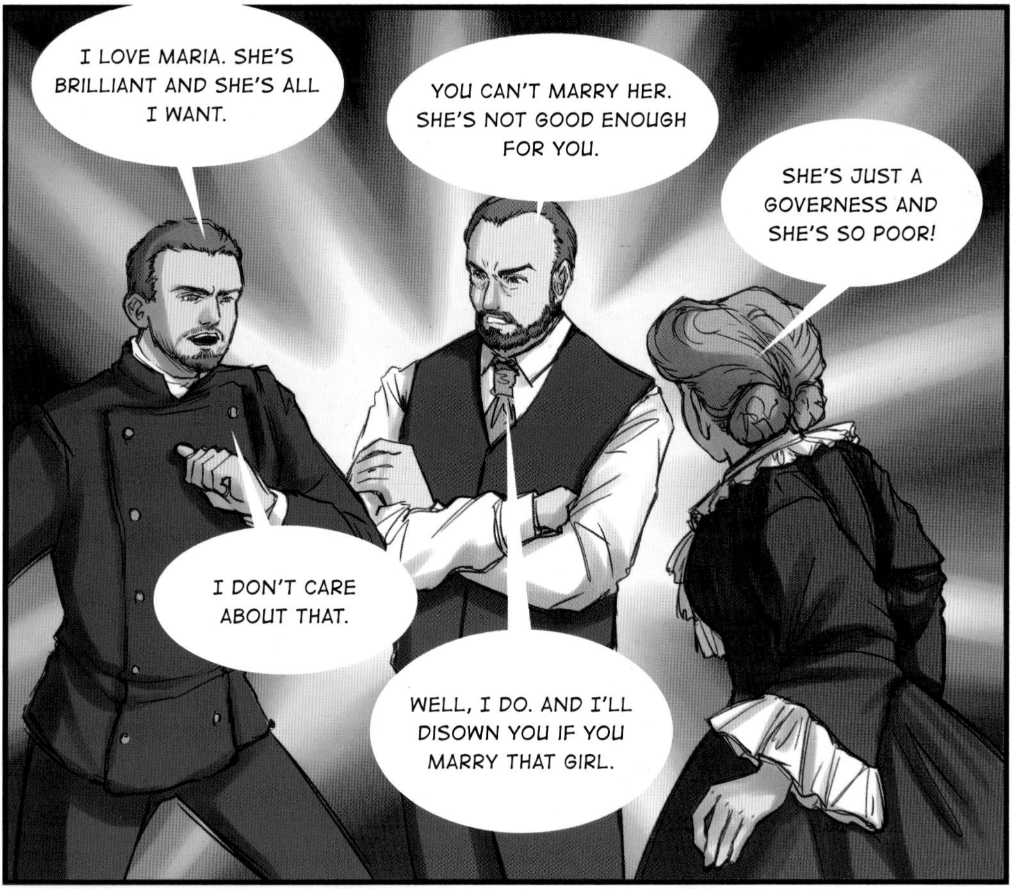
I LOVE MARIA. SHE'S BRILLIANT AND SHE'S ALL I WANT.
YOU CAN'T MARRY HER. SHE'S NOT GOOD ENOUGH FOR YOU.
SHE'S JUST A GOVERNESS AND SHE'S SO POOR!
I DON'T CARE ABOUT THAT.
WELL, I DO. AND I'LL DISOWN YOU IF YOU MARRY THAT GIRL.

THE ROMANCE DRAGGED ON FOR A FEW YEARS, BUT ENDED UNHAPPILY. KAZIMIERZ OBEYED HIS PARENTS AND DID NOT MARRY MARIA.

MARIA, HURT AND HUMILIATED, HAD TO CONTINUE WORKING FOR THE ŻÓRAWSKIS BECAUSE SHE NEEDED THE MONEY TO SEND TO BRONIA. BUT SHE CARRIED ON WITH HER STUDIES AND GREW USED TO WORKING ALONE.

I WON'T LET MYSELF BE BEATEN DOWN.

IN 1889, MARIA'S EMPLOYMENT WITH THE ŻÓRAWSKIS FINALLY CAME TO AN END. SHE WORKED AS A GOVERNESS FOR ANOTHER YEAR IN WARSAW AND KEPT SENDING MONEY TO HER SISTER. OF COURSE, SHE NEVER STOPPED STUDYING.

THEN, EXCITINGLY, ONE OF HER COUSINS CREATED WHAT HE CALLED WARSAW'S MUSEUM OF INDUSTRY AND AGRICULTURE. THE RUSSIANS DIDN'T KNOW IT, BUT IT WAS ACTUALLY A LAB WHERE POLISH STUDENTS COULD SECRETLY STUDY SCIENCE.

I CAN'T BELIEVE I CAN FINALLY WORK IN A REAL LAB! I WANT TO TRY OUT THESE EXPERIMENTS I'VE ONLY READ ABOUT.

THERE'S A LETTER FROM BRONIA. SHE'S DONE WITH HER STUDIES AND SHE'S GETTING MARRIED TO A FELLOW DOCTOR. HIS NAME IS KAZIMIERZ DŁUSKI.

AND SHE'S INVITING ME TO LIVE WITH HER IN PARIS SO I CAN ATTEND THE SORBONNE.

CHAPTER 4

PARIS AT LAST

IN NOVEMBER 1891, AFTER WORKING FOR SEVEN YEARS, THE ALMOST TWENTY-FOUR-YEAR-OLD MARIA BOARDED A TRAIN TO PARIS.

I'LL BE GONE ONLY A FEW YEARS. ONCE I PASS MY EXAMS, I'LL RETURN HOME AND BECOME A TEACHER.

COME BACK QUICKLY, MY DEAR!

TO SAVE MONEY, SHE BOUGHT A FOURTH-CLASS TICKET. THERE WAS NO SEAT, SO SHE SAT ON A STOOL SHE BROUGHT ALONG, AND KEPT WARM BY WRAPPING HERSELF IN HER OWN BLANKETS.

AFTER AN EXHAUSTING THREE-DAY JOURNEY, MARIA FINALLY ARRIVED AT THE PLACE SHE HAD DREAMED OF FOR SO LONG.

YOU MUST BE BRONIA'S HUSBAND.

PARIS, THE CAPITAL OF FRANCE, WAS VERY DIFFERENT FROM WARSAW. THE WORLD'S TALLEST STRUCTURE AT THE TIME, THE EIFFEL TOWER, HAD JUST BEEN BUILT. BRAND-NEW ELECTRIC STREETLAMPS LINED SOME OF THE STREETS, REPLACING OLD-FASHIONED GASLIGHTS. RESTAURANTS AND CAFÉS WERE EVERYWHERE, AND FASHIONABLE PEOPLE STROLLED THE STREETS. EVERYTHING WAS SO EXCITING AND NEW!

WELCOME TO PARIS, MARIA!

MARIA PROMPTLY ENROLLED IN CLASSES AT THE SORBONNE, THE MOST FAMOUS UNIVERSITY IN FRANCE. SHE WAS ONE OF TWENTY-THREE WOMEN AMONG OVER 1,800 STUDENTS ENROLLED IN THE FACULTÉ DES SCIENCES.

USING THE FRENCH VERSION OF HER NAME, SHE REGISTERED AS MARIE, NOT MARIA.

IT TOOK MARIE ABOUT AN HOUR TRAVELING BY HORSE-DRAWN BUS TO GET FROM HER SISTER'S RESIDENCE TO THE SORBONNE.

BRONIA AND HER HUSBAND'S HOME WAS VERY BUSY AND RARELY QUIET. THEY USED THEIR APARTMENT AS THEIR MEDICAL OFFICES. IN THE EVENINGS, THEY ENTERTAINED OTHER POLES LIVING IN FRANCE AND DISCUSSED PATRIOTIC MATTERS. ARTISTS, MUSICIANS, SCIENTISTS, AND POLISH ACTIVISTS WERE ALL WELCOME.

COME IN, COME IN! PUT SOME MORE TEA ON, BRONIA. MARIA, LEAVE THOSE BOOKS ALONE FOR A MINUTE AND JOIN THE PARTY.

I CAN'T CONCENTRATE WITH ALL THE NOISE!

BRONIA, I'M SPENDING TWO HOURS A DAY JUST TRAVELING AND WASTING ALL THIS MONEY ON BUS RIDES. I'M GOING TO LOOK FOR AN APARTMENT CLOSER TO THE UNIVERSITY.

I UNDERSTAND, BUT I SHALL MISS YOU—AND YOU KNOW YOU'RE ALWAYS WELCOME HERE.

AFTER A FEW MONTHS, MARIE SET OFF ON HER OWN. SHE HAD LITTLE MONEY, SO SHE LIVED AS CHEAPLY AS SHE COULD. SHE RENTED A TINY, UNHEATED ATTIC, SIX FLIGHTS UP.

I'LL FINALLY HAVE SOME QUIET SO I CAN STUDY IN PEACE!

SOMETIMES IT WAS SO COLD SHE SLEPT WITH ALL HER CLOTHES PILED ON TOP OF HER.

THE WATER FROZE IN HER WASHBASIN.

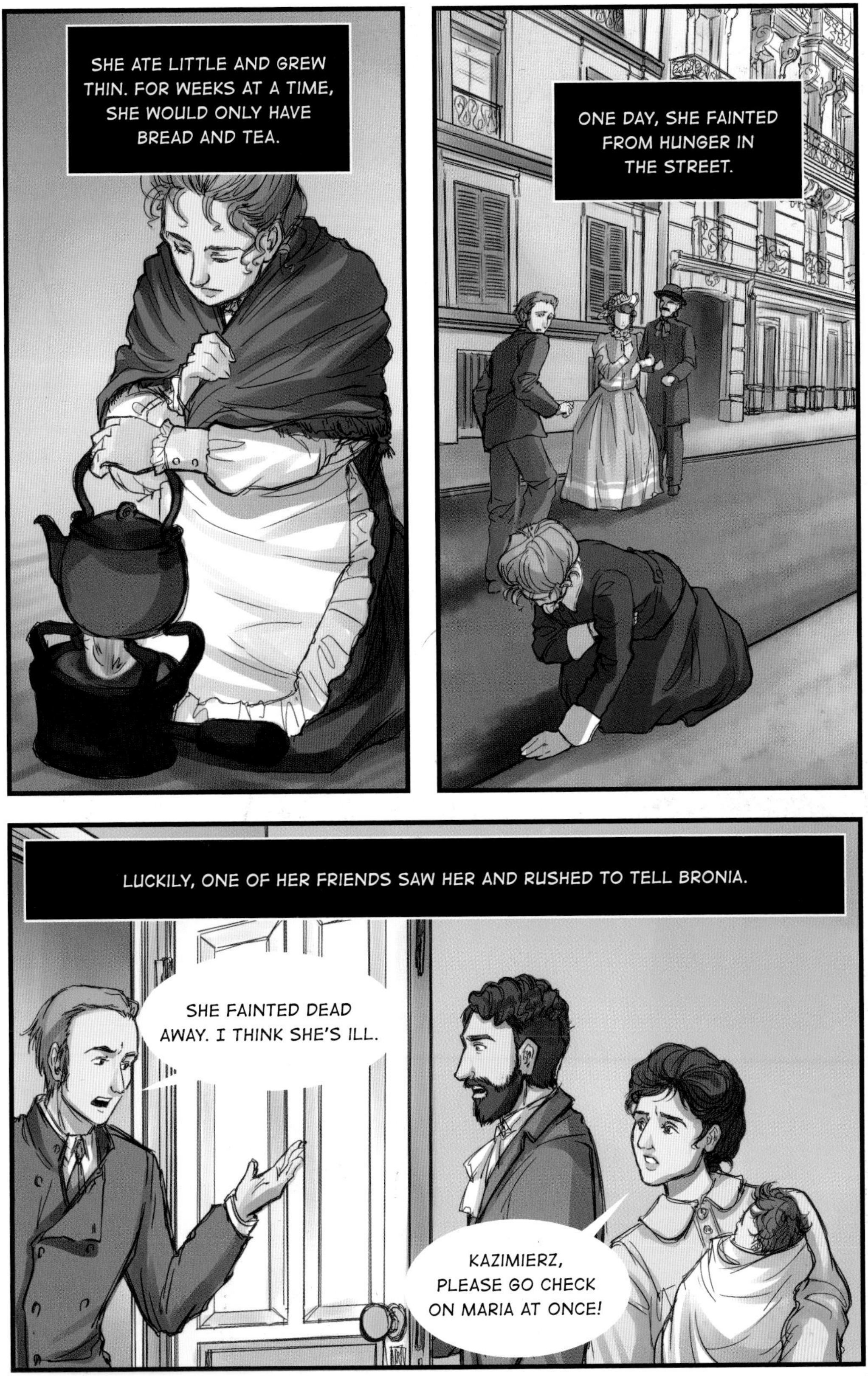
SHE ATE LITTLE AND GREW THIN. FOR WEEKS AT A TIME, SHE WOULD ONLY HAVE BREAD AND TEA.
ONE DAY, SHE FAINTED FROM HUNGER IN THE STREET.
LUCKILY, ONE OF HER FRIENDS SAW HER AND RUSHED TO TELL BRONIA.
SHE FAINTED DEAD AWAY. I THINK SHE'S ILL.
KAZIMIERZ, PLEASE GO CHECK ON MARIA AT ONCE!

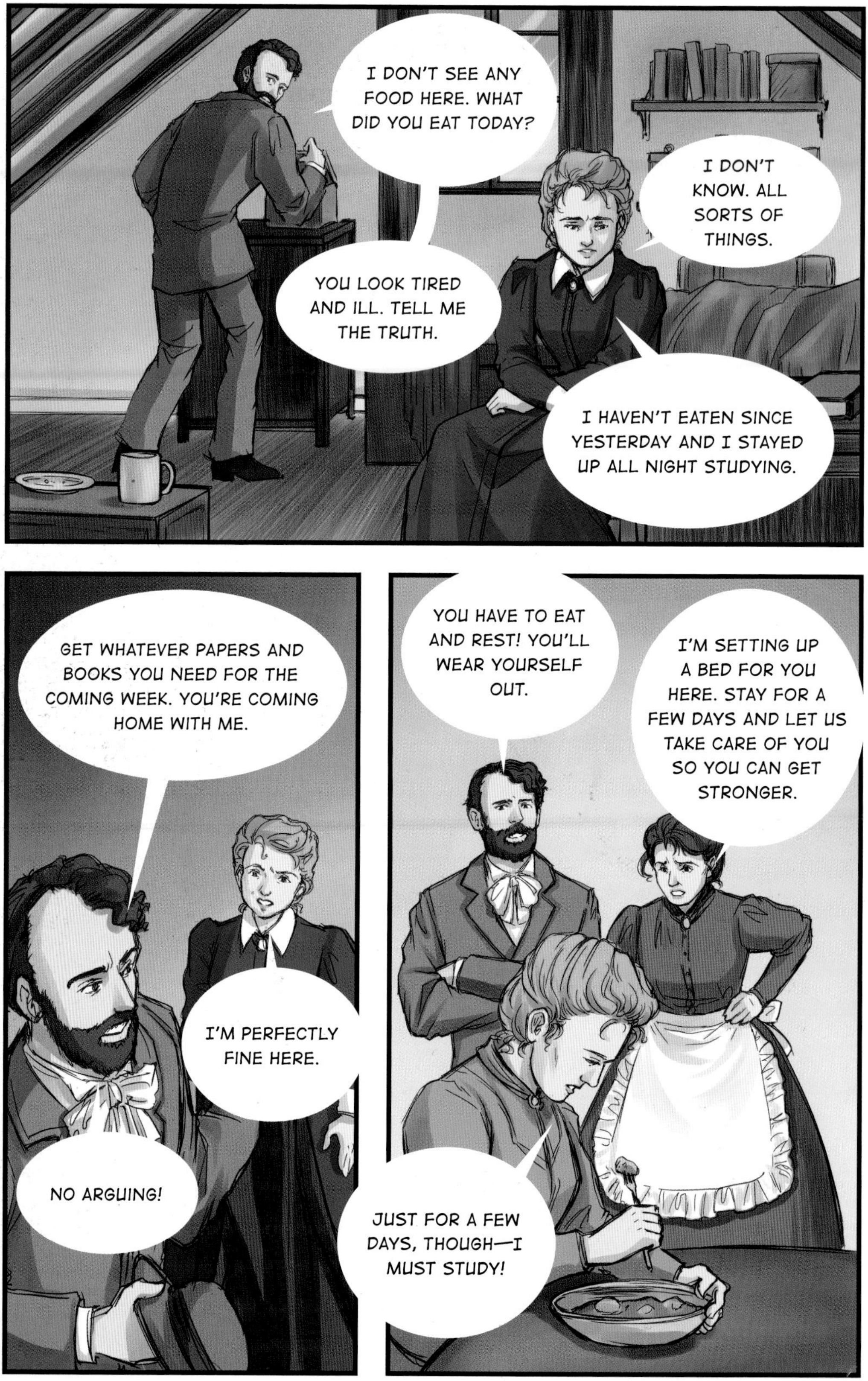
I DON'T SEE ANY FOOD HERE. WHAT DID YOU EAT TODAY?
I DON'T KNOW. ALL SORTS OF THINGS.
YOU LOOK TIRED AND ILL. TELL ME THE TRUTH.
I HAVEN'T EATEN SINCE YESTERDAY AND I STAYED UP ALL NIGHT STUDYING.
GET WHATEVER PAPERS AND BOOKS YOU NEED FOR THE COMING WEEK. YOU'RE COMING HOME WITH ME.
I'M PERFECTLY FINE HERE.
NO ARGUING!
YOU HAVE TO EAT AND REST! YOU'LL WEAR YOURSELF OUT.
I'M SETTING UP A BED FOR YOU HERE. STAY FOR A FEW DAYS AND LET US TAKE CARE OF YOU SO YOU CAN GET STRONGER.
JUST FOR A FEW DAYS, THOUGH—I MUST STUDY!

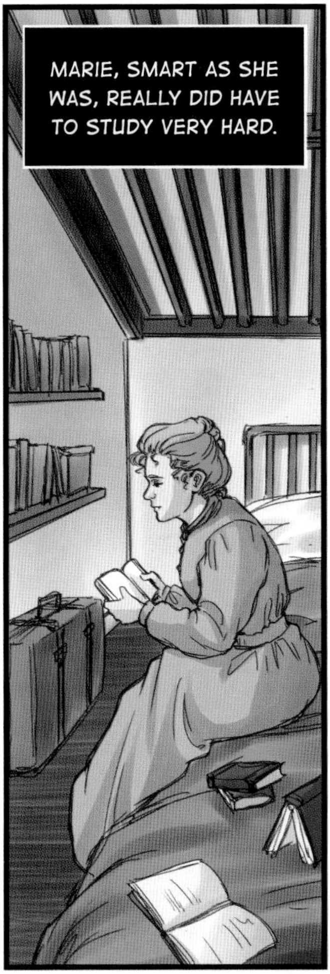
MARIE, SMART AS SHE WAS, REALLY DID HAVE TO STUDY VERY HARD.

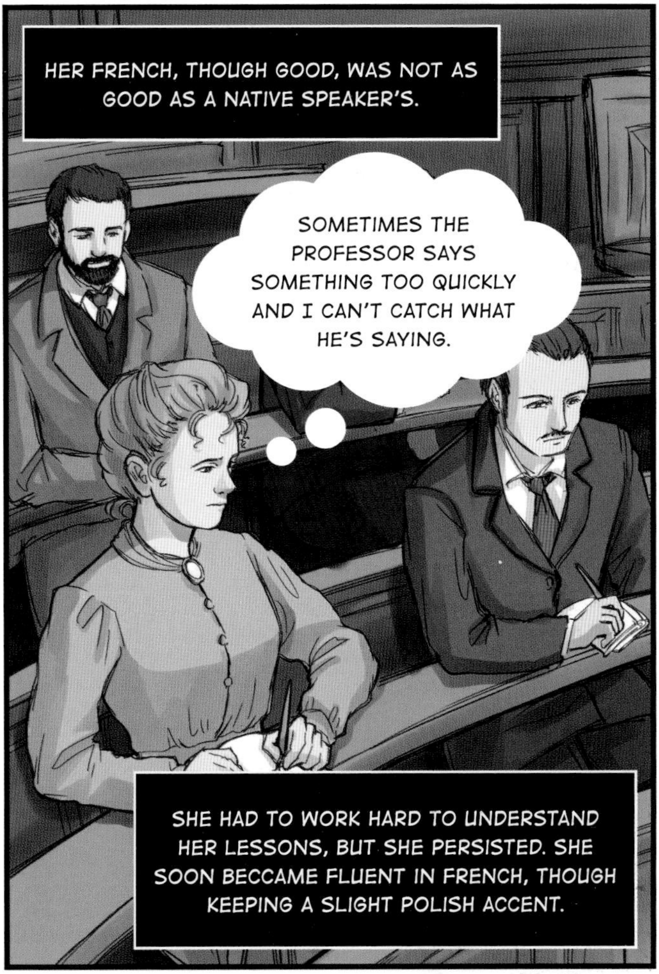
HER FRENCH, THOUGH GOOD, WAS NOT AS GOOD AS A NATIVE SPEAKER'S.
SOMETIMES THE PROFESSOR SAYS SOMETHING TOO QUICKLY AND I CAN'T CATCH WHAT HE'S SAYING.
SHE HAD TO WORK HARD TO UNDERSTAND HER LESSONS, BUT SHE PERSISTED. SHE SOON BECCAME FLUENT IN FRENCH, THOUGH KEEPING A SLIGHT POLISH ACCENT.

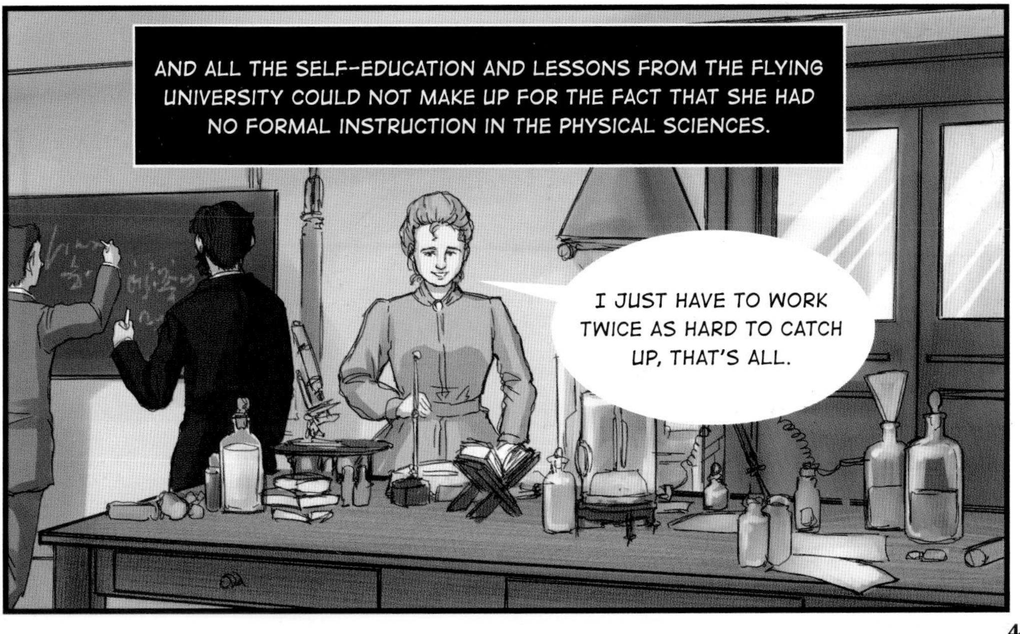
AND ALL THE SELF-EDUCATION AND LESSONS FROM THE FLYING UNIVERSITY COULD NOT MAKE UP FOR THE FACT THAT SHE HAD NO FORMAL INSTRUCTION IN THE PHYSICAL SCIENCES.
I JUST HAVE TO WORK TWICE AS HARD TO CATCH UP, THAT'S ALL.

MARIE DIVIDED HER TIME BETWEEN HER COURSES, HER LAB WORK, AND STUDYING AT THE UNIVERSITY LIBRARY.

EVEN WITH ALL THE HARDSHIPS, MARIE WAS HAPPY. SHE WAS FREE TO STUDY EVERYTHING SHE WANTED TO LEARN, TO HER HEART'S CONTENT—WITHOUT SPIES, WITHOUT RESTRICTIONS, AND WITHOUT THE FEAR OF BEING ARRESTED.

"ALL THAT I SAW AND LEARNED THAT WAS NEW DELIGHTED ME. IT WAS LIKE A NEW WORLD OPENED TO ME, THE WORLD OF SCIENCE, WHICH I WAS AT LAST PERMITTED TO KNOW IN ALL LIBERTY."

MARIE'S TEACHERS AT THE SORBONNE WERE AMONG THE BEST IN THE WORLD.

HER PHYSICS PROFESSOR WAS FUTURE NOBEL PRIZE WINNER GABRIEL LIPPMANN, WHO WAS TO INVENT COLOR PHOTOGRAPHY.

ÉMILE DUCLAUX, A CUTTING-EDGE RESEARCHER, WAS HER BIOCHEMISTRY PROFESSOR.

HER MATHEMATICS TEACHER WAS HENRI POINCARÉ, THE GREATEST MATHEMATICIAN OF HIS DAY.

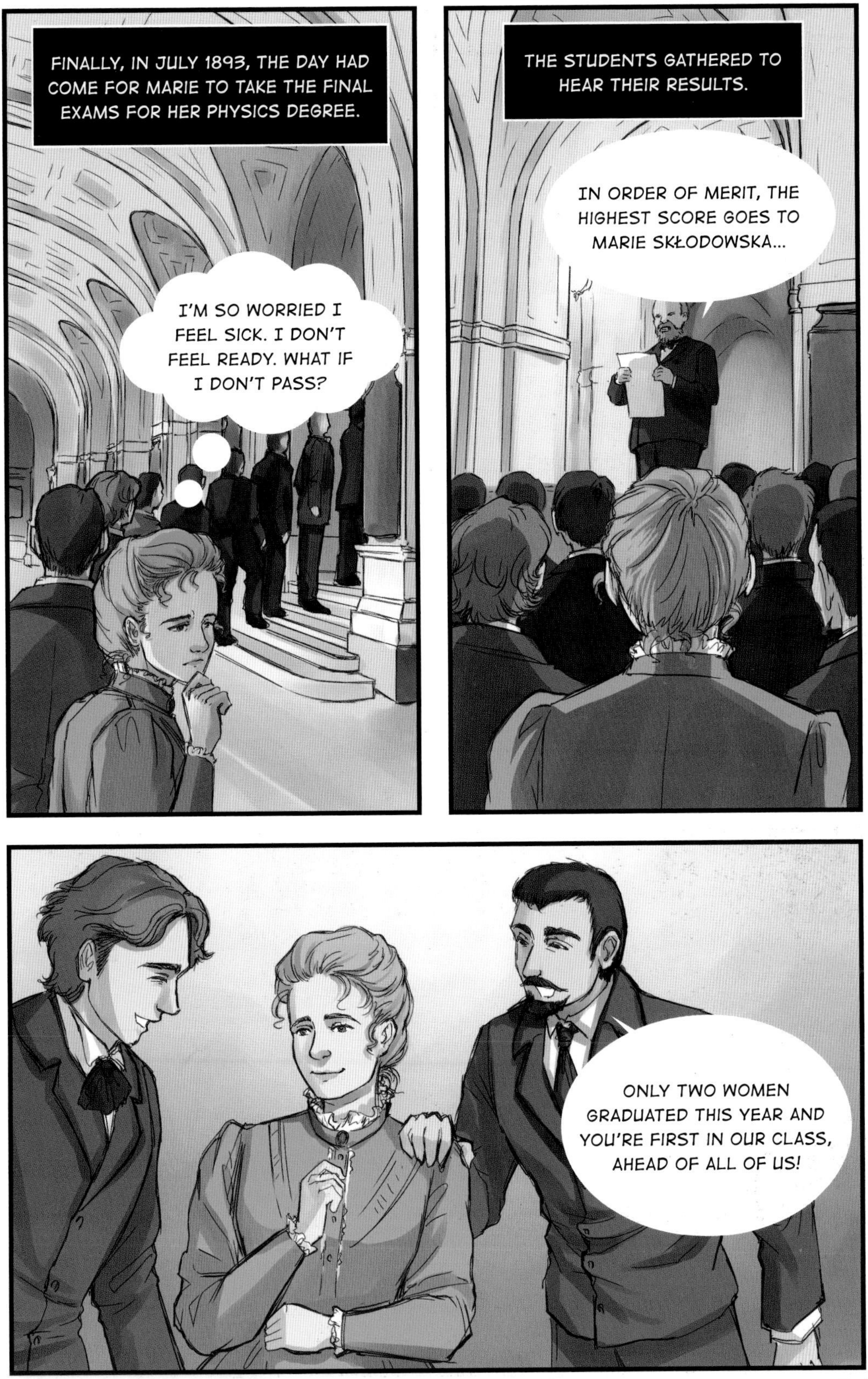
FINALLY, IN JULY 1893, THE DAY HAD COME FOR MARIE TO TAKE THE FINAL EXAMS FOR HER PHYSICS DEGREE.
I'M SO WORRIED I FEEL SICK. I DON'T FEEL READY. WHAT IF I DON'T PASS?
THE STUDENTS GATHERED TO HEAR THEIR RESULTS.
IN ORDER OF MERIT, THE HIGHEST SCORE GOES TO MARIE SKŁODOWSKA...
ONLY TWO WOMEN GRADUATED THIS YEAR AND YOU'RE FIRST IN OUR CLASS, AHEAD OF ALL OF US!

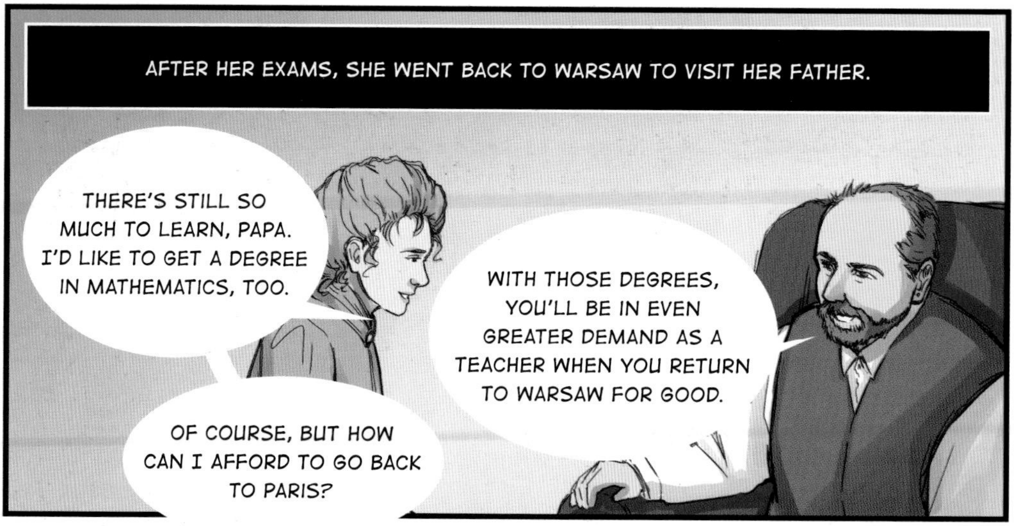
AFTER HER EXAMS, SHE WENT BACK TO WARSAW TO VISIT HER FATHER.
THERE'S STILL SO MUCH TO LEARN, PAPA. I'D LIKE TO GET A DEGREE IN MATHEMATICS, TOO.
WITH THOSE DEGREES, YOU'LL BE IN EVEN GREATER DEMAND AS A TEACHER WHEN YOU RETURN TO WARSAW FOR GOOD.
OF COURSE, BUT HOW CAN I AFFORD TO GO BACK TO PARIS?

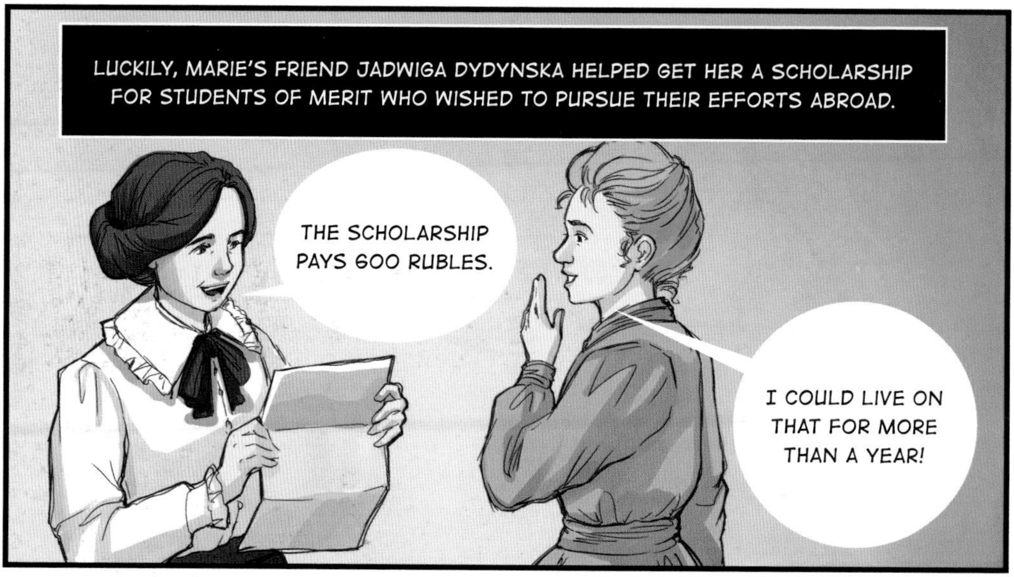
LUCKILY, MARIE'S FRIEND JADWIGA DYDYNSKA HELPED GET HER A SCHOLARSHIP FOR STUDENTS OF MERIT WHO WISHED TO PURSUE THEIR EFFORTS ABROAD.
THE SCHOLARSHIP PAYS 600 RUBLES.
I COULD LIVE ON THAT FOR MORE THAN A YEAR!

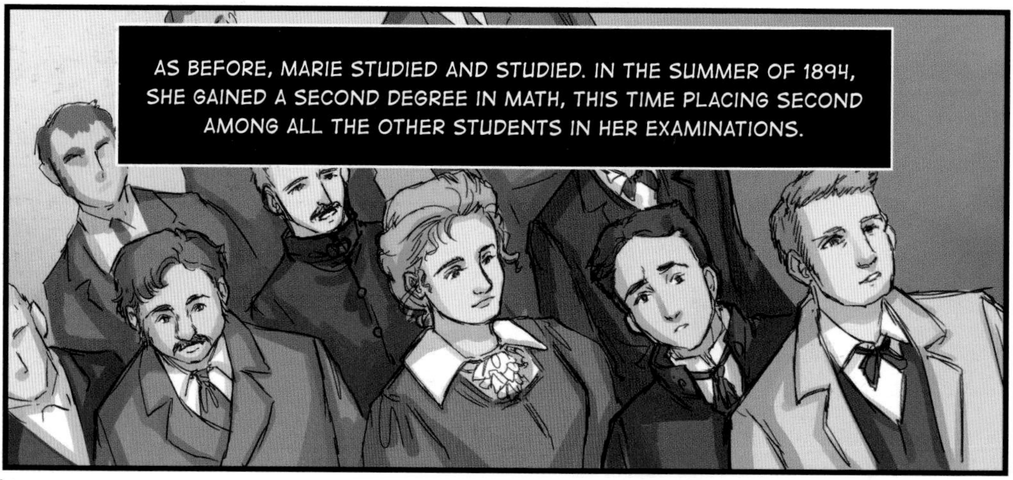
AS BEFORE, MARIE STUDIED AND STUDIED. IN THE SUMMER OF 1894, SHE GAINED A SECOND DEGREE IN MATH, THIS TIME PLACING SECOND AMONG ALL THE OTHER STUDENTS IN HER EXAMINATIONS.

WHILE MARIE WAS STUDYING FOR HER MATH DEGREE, THE SOCIETY FOR THE ENCOURAGEMENT OF NATIONAL INDUSTRY OFFERED HER A JOB TO RESEARCH MAGNETISM IN STEEL. SHE WAS WORKING IN THE LAB OF ONE OF HER TEACHERS, GABRIEL LIPPMANN.

IT'S SO CROWDED—I CAN'T GET GOOD RESULTS HERE.

SO TO DO MY RESEARCH ON MAGNETISM, I NEED TO FIND A BETTER LAB.

MARIE MET A POLISH PHYSICIST NAMED JÓZEF WIERUSZ-KOWALSKI WHO WAS VISITING PARIS.

I KNOW PIERRE CURIE HAS DONE WORK ON MAGNETISM. HE'S HEAD OF THE LABS AT THE MUNICIPAL SCHOOL OF INDUSTRIAL PHYSICS AND CHEMISTRY HERE IN PARIS. IT'S NOT THE SORBONNE, BUT PERHAPS HE HAS SOME LAB SPACE? I'LL ARRANGE A MEETING IF YOU'D LIKE.

IF YOU THINK HE COULD HELP...

CHAPTER 5

A PERFECT UNION

IN THE SPRING OF 1894, KOWALSKI INVITED MARIE AND PIERRE TO TEA.

MARIE SKŁODOWSKA, MAY I INTRODUCE YOU TO PIERRE CURIE.

PIERRE WAS THIRTY-FIVE YEARS OLD, NINE YEARS OLDER THAN MARIE.

A FRENCH SCIENTIST, HE WAS KNOWN FOR HIS WORK ON CRYSTALS, ELECTRICITY, AND MAGNETISM.

MOSTLY EDUCATED AT HOME BY HIS FATHER EUGENE, A DOCTOR, PIERRE SHOWED PROMISE IN MATH AND SCIENCE.

IN 1880, HE AND HIS OLDER BROTHER JACQUES DISCOVERED PIEZOELECTRICITY. THEY SHOWED THAT APPLYING PRESSURE TO CERTAIN CRYSTALS CREATED AN ELECTRIC CHARGE.

PIERRE AND JACQUES INVENTED A SENSITIVE LAB APPARATUS, A PIEZOELECTRIC QUARTZ ELECTROMETER. THIS BECAME KNOWN AS THE CURIE ELECTROMETER IN FRANCE.

LATER PIERRE TURNED HIS ATTENTION TO MAGNETISM. HE SHOWED THAT THE MAGNETIC PROPERTIES OF A SUBSTANCE CHANGED AT A CERTAIN TEMPERATURE. THIS TEMPERATURE IS NOW KNOWN AS THE CURIE POINT.

FOR PIERRE, AS FOR MARIE, SCIENCE MEANT EVERYTHING. ONE DAY HE WAS WORKING OUT A PROBLEM WITH TWO OF HIS STUDENTS AND LOST TRACK OF THE TIME. THEY ENDED UP LOCKED IN THE CLASSROOM AND HAD TO CLIMB OUT A WINDOW TO ESCAPE!

MARIE WROTE OF MEETING PIERRE FOR THE FIRST TIME:

"WE BEGAN A CONVERSATION, WHICH SOON BECAME FRIENDLY. IT FIRST CONCERNED CERTAIN SCIENTIFIC MATTERS, WHICH I WAS GLAD TO BE ABLE TO ASK HIS OPINION. THEN WE DISCUSSED CERTAIN SOCIAL AND HUMANITARIAN SUBJECTS THAT INTERESTED US BOTH."

WE HAVE SO MANY THINGS IN COMMON. COULD WE MEET AGAIN?

I'D LIKE THAT.

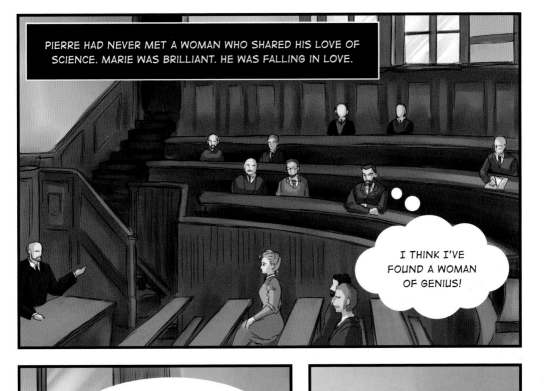

PIERRE HAD NEVER MET A WOMAN WHO SHARED HIS LOVE OF SCIENCE. MARIE WAS BRILLIANT. HE WAS FALLING IN LOVE.

I THINK I'VE FOUND A WOMAN OF GENIUS!

IT'S FROM PIERRE! A COPY OF HIS LATEST SCIENTIFIC PAPER, AND HE'S SCRIBBLED A DEDICATION TO ME:

"TO MADEMOISELLE SKŁODOWSKA, WITH THE RESPECT AND FRIENDSHIP OF THE AUTHOR, P. CURIE."

THIS IS SO MUCH BETTER THAN GETTING CHOCOLATE OR FLOWERS!

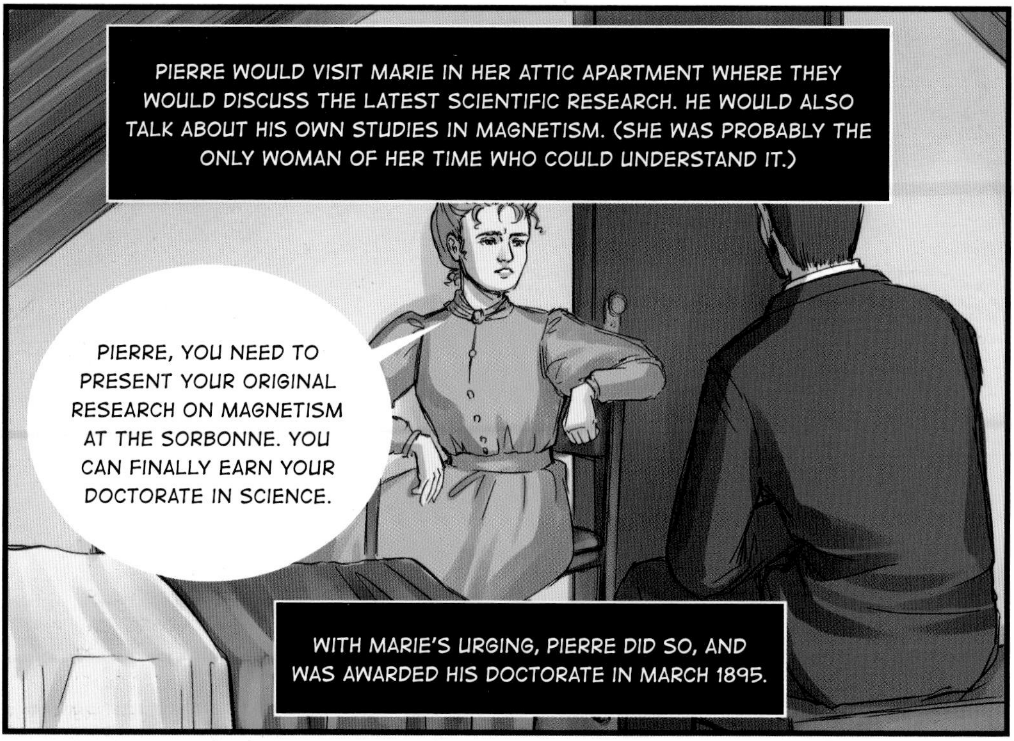
PIERRE WOULD VISIT MARIE IN HER ATTIC APARTMENT WHERE THEY WOULD DISCUSS THE LATEST SCIENTIFIC RESEARCH. HE WOULD ALSO TALK ABOUT HIS OWN STUDIES IN MAGNETISM. (SHE WAS PROBABLY THE ONLY WOMAN OF HER TIME WHO COULD UNDERSTAND IT.)
PIERRE, YOU NEED TO PRESENT YOUR ORIGINAL RESEARCH ON MAGNETISM AT THE SORBONNE. YOU CAN FINALLY EARN YOUR DOCTORATE IN SCIENCE.
WITH MARIE'S URGING, PIERRE DID SO, AND WAS AWARDED HIS DOCTORATE IN MARCH 1895.

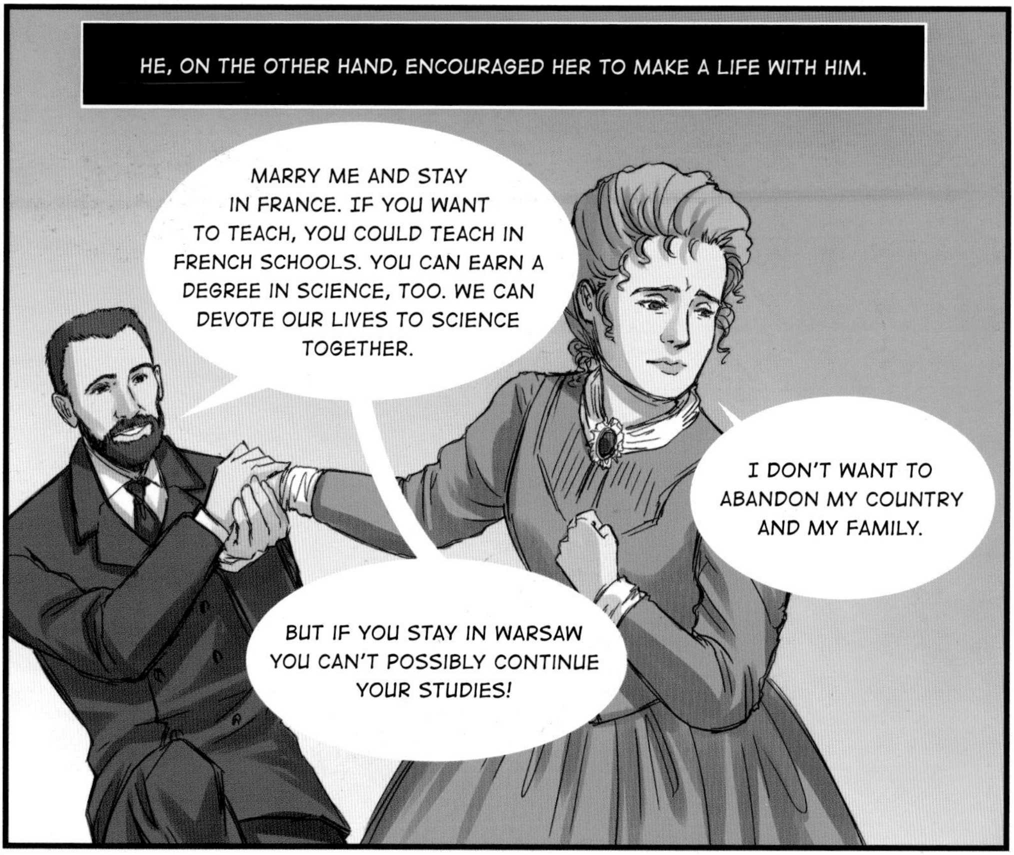
HE, ON THE OTHER HAND, ENCOURAGED HER TO MAKE A LIFE WITH HIM.
MARRY ME AND STAY IN FRANCE. IF YOU WANT TO TEACH, YOU COULD TEACH IN FRENCH SCHOOLS. YOU CAN EARN A DEGREE IN SCIENCE, TOO. WE CAN DEVOTE OUR LIVES TO SCIENCE TOGETHER.
I DON'T WANT TO ABANDON MY COUNTRY AND MY FAMILY.
BUT IF YOU STAY IN WARSAW YOU CAN'T POSSIBLY CONTINUE YOUR STUDIES!

IN THE SUMMER OF 1894, AFTER HER MATHEMATICS EXAMINATION, MARIE RETURNED TO WARSAW TO STAY WITH HER FATHER.

MORE LETTERS FROM PIERRE? HE'S VERY PERSISTENT.

I'M JUST NOT SURE WHAT TO DO, PAPA.

"IT WOULD BE A FINE THING...TO PASS OUR LIVES NEAR EACH OTHER, HYPNOTIZED BY OUR DREAMS: YOUR PATRIOTIC DREAM, OUR HUMANITARIAN DREAM, AND OUR SCIENTIFIC DREAM..."

IN OCTOBER 1894, MARIE RETURNED TO FRANCE AND THE SORBONNE TO CONTINUE HER STUDIES. PIERRE CONTINUED TO BEG HER TO MARRY HIM IN THE FOLLOWING MONTHS.

WHAT IF I WENT TO WARSAW AND GOT A POSITION THERE?

WOULD YOU MARRY ME THEN? I COULD GIVE FRENCH LESSONS AND WITH WHATEVER WE MAKE, WE'LL CONTINUE OUR SCIENTIFIC RESEARCH.

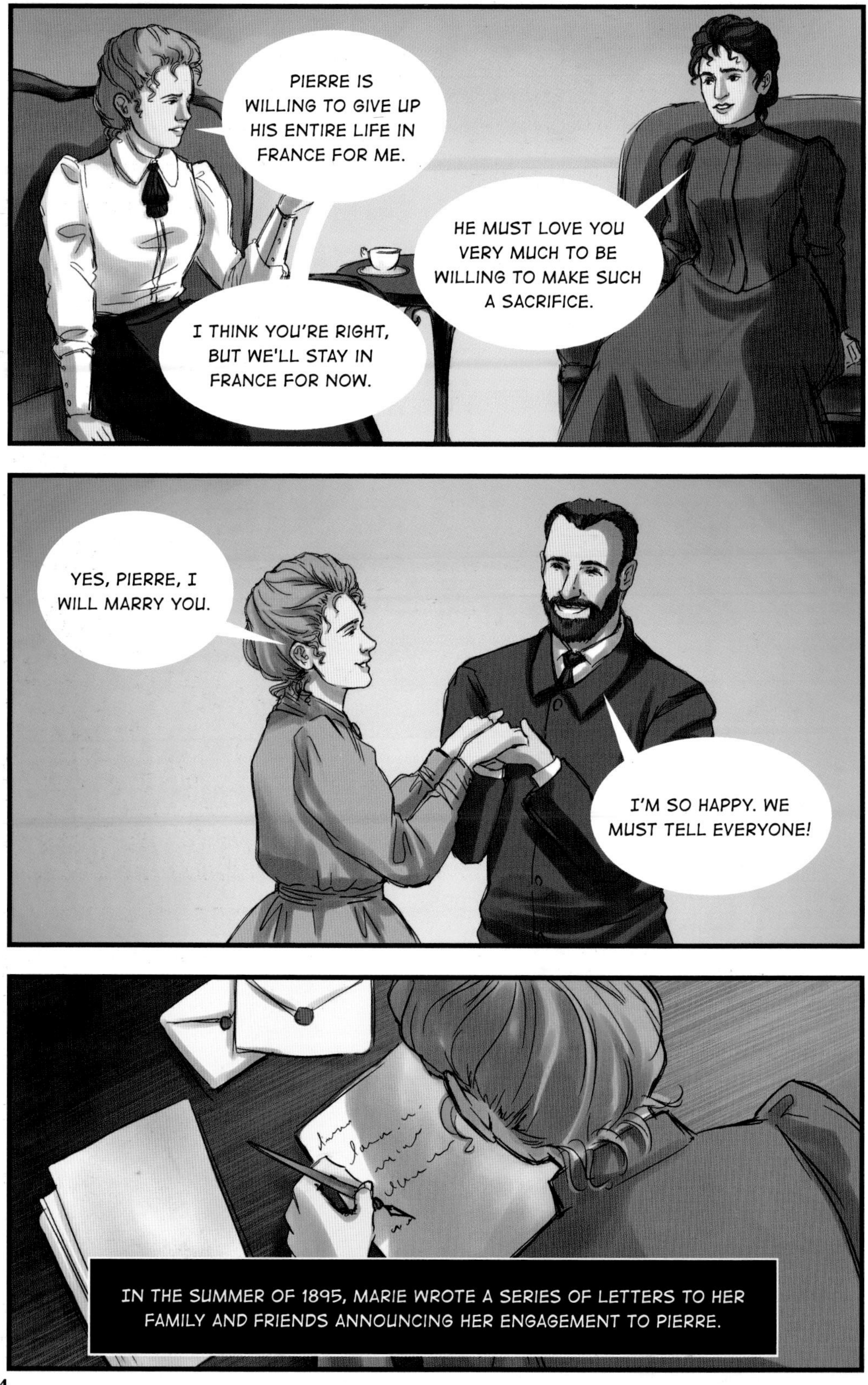
PIERRE IS WILLING TO GIVE UP HIS ENTIRE LIFE IN FRANCE FOR ME.
HE MUST LOVE YOU VERY MUCH TO BE WILLING TO MAKE SUCH A SACRIFICE.
I THINK YOU'RE RIGHT, BUT WE'LL STAY IN FRANCE FOR NOW.
YES, PIERRE, I WILL MARRY YOU.
I'M SO HAPPY. WE MUST TELL EVERYONE!
IN THE SUMMER OF 1895, MARIE WROTE A SERIES OF LETTERS TO HER FAMILY AND FRIENDS ANNOUNCING HER ENGAGEMENT TO PIERRE.

SHE WROTE TO HER OLDER BROTHER, JÓZEF, NOW A DOCTOR IN WARSAW, THAT SHE WAS WORRIED ABOUT NOT RETURNING TO HELP POLAND AND THEIR FATHER.

AM I BEING DISLOYAL TO MY COUNTRY?

"I THINK YOU ARE RIGHT TO FOLLOW YOUR HEART, AND NO JUST PERSON CAN REPROACH YOU FOR IT. KNOWING YOU, I AM CONVINCED THAT YOU WILL REMAIN POLISH WITH ALL YOUR SOUL, AND ALSO THAT YOU WILL NEVER CEASE TO BE PART OF OUR FAMILY IN YOUR HEART."

"I'D RATHER SEE YOU HAPPY AND CONTENTED IN PARIS THAN BACK AGAIN IN OUR COUNTRY, BROKEN BY SACRIFICE AND A VICTIM OF WHAT YOU THINK IS YOUR DUTY."

"IT IS A SORROW TO ME TO HAVE TO STAY FOREVER IN FRANCE, BUT WHAT AM I TO DO? FATE HAS MADE US DEEPLY ATTACHED TO EACH OTHER AND WE CANNOT ENDURE THE IDEA OF SEPARATING...WHEN YOU RECEIVE THIS LETTER WRITE TO ME: MADAME CURIE, SCHOOL OF PHYSICS AND CHEMISTRY, 42 RUE LHOMOND."

MARIE ALSO WROTE TO HER FRIEND KAZIA.

MY DEAR MARIA IS GETTING MARRIED! SHE'LL NOW BE MADAME CURIE!

MARIE AND PIERRE PLANNED THEIR WEDDING. THEY WANTED SOMETHING VERY SIMPLE: NO RINGS, NO WHITE DRESS, AND NO EXTRAVAGANT CHURCH CEREMONY.

YOUR MOTHER-IN-LAW IS MAKING YOU A PRESENT OF YOUR WEDDING DRESS. WHAT WOULD YOU LIKE?

OH, NOTHING FANCY! I WANT SOMETHING PRACTICAL AND DARK THAT I'LL BE ABLE TO WEAR AGAIN WHEN I WORK IN THE LAB.

ON JULY 26, 1895, IN A CIVIL CEREMONY, PIERRE AND MARIE EXCHANGED THEIR VOWS.

PIERRE'S PARENTS HELD A WEDDING PARTY FOR THE HAPPY COUPLE AT THEIR HOUSE IN SCEAUX, NEAR PARIS. MARIE'S FATHER AND HER SISTER HELENA HAD COME ALL THE WAY FROM WARSAW TO ATTEND.

I WISH YOU ALL THE HAPPINESS IN THE WORLD, MY DEAR.

AFTER THE WEDDING, MARIE AND PIERRE SET OFF ON A BICYCLING HONEYMOON. THEY ENJOYED RIDING THROUGH THE FRENCH COUNTRYSIDE OF BRITTANY, AND FELL MORE AND MORE IN LOVE.

ISN'T THIS A GLORIOUS DAY? I LOVE BEING IN THE COUNTRY!

SO DO I!

IN THE MIDDLE OF AUGUST, THEY VISITED BRONIA AND KAZIMIERZ WHO HAD RENTED A FARMHOUSE FOR A FEW MONTHS NEAR CHANTILLY, FRANCE. MARIE'S FATHER AND SISTER WERE THERE AS WELL, EXTENDING THEIR STAY IN FRANCE.

I'M TRYING TO LEARN POLISH FOR MARIE.

I'M DELIGHTED, BUT GOOD LUCK! POLISH IS VERY HARD!

AND IN SEPTEMBER, THEY VISITED PIERRE'S PARENTS.

THEY ARE SO IMPRESSED BY YOU—THEY LOVE YOU ALREADY.

AND I LOVE THEM—THEY'VE BEEN SO KIND TO ME.

IN OCTOBER, THEY SETTLED INTO A SMALL APARTMENT NEAR PIERRE'S SCHOOL.

MY PARENTS SAY WE CAN TAKE ANOTHER CHAIR FROM SCEAUX IF WE NEED ONE.

NO, I DON'T WANT A LOT OF FURNITURE. THERE'S JUST MORE TO DUST AND CLEAN. I WANT TO CONCENTRATE ON MY WORK.

AND MARIE, AS ALWAYS, HAD A LOT OF WORK TO DO. SHE CONTINUED HER RESEARCH ON MAGNETISM AND STEEL IN PIERRE'S LAB.

SHE ATTENDED LECTURES AT THE SORBONNE.

MARIE WAS ALSO STUDYING FOR YET ANOTHER EXAMINATION.

IF I PASS, I'LL BE ABLE TO TEACH SCIENCE TO HIGH-SCHOOL GIRLS IN FRENCH SCHOOLS.

SHE PASSED THE EXAM AT THE TOP OF HER CLASS IN THE SUMMER OF 1896.

MARIE ALSO DID THE COOKING AND HOUSEKEEPING.

SOON THERE WOULD BE EVEN MORE FOR HER TO DO WITH AN ADDITION TO THE FAMILY.

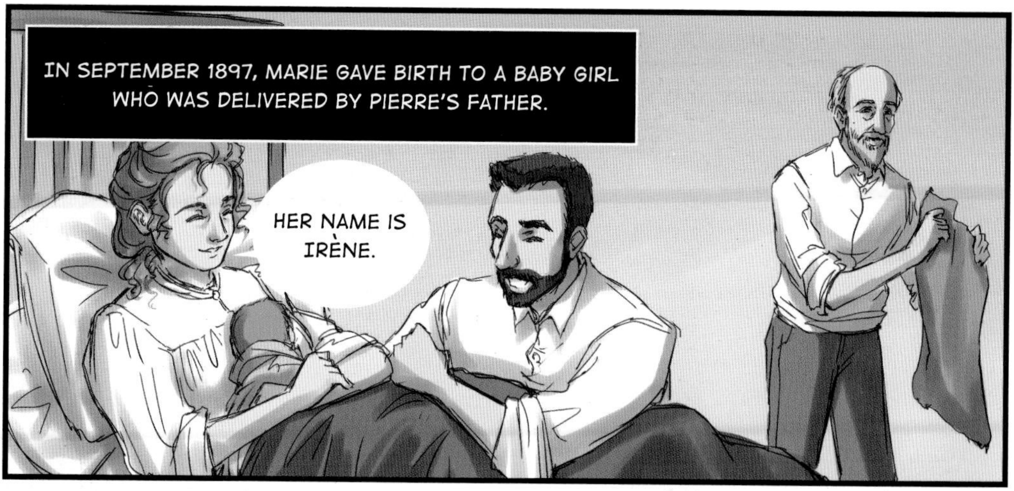
IN SEPTEMBER 1897, MARIE GAVE BIRTH TO A BABY GIRL WHO WAS DELIVERED BY PIERRE'S FATHER.
HER NAME IS IRÈNE.

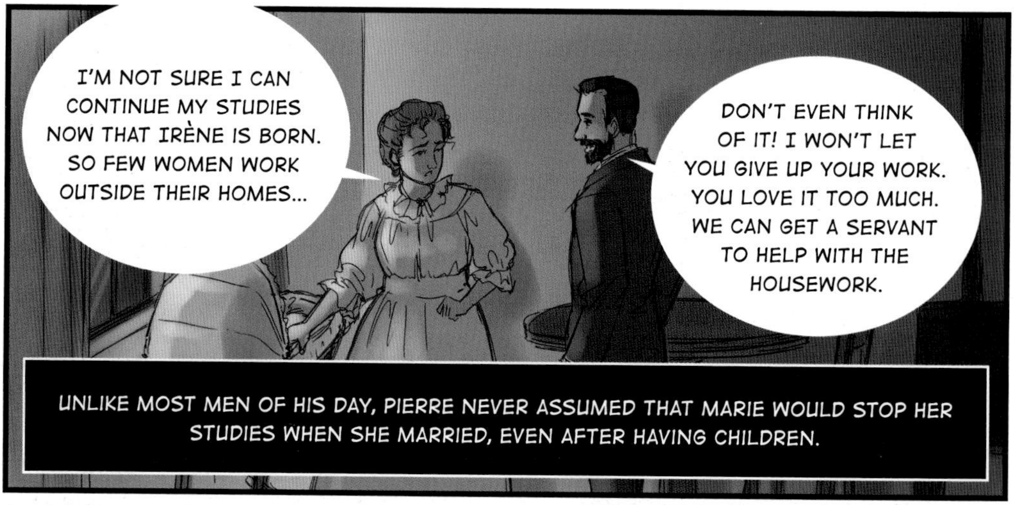
I'M NOT SURE I CAN CONTINUE MY STUDIES NOW THAT IRÈNE IS BORN. SO FEW WOMEN WORK OUTSIDE THEIR HOMES...
DON'T EVEN THINK OF IT! I WON'T LET YOU GIVE UP YOUR WORK. YOU LOVE IT TOO MUCH. WE CAN GET A SERVANT TO HELP WITH THE HOUSEWORK.
UNLIKE MOST MEN OF HIS DAY, PIERRE NEVER ASSUMED THAT MARIE WOULD STOP HER STUDIES WHEN SHE MARRIED, EVEN AFTER HAVING CHILDREN.

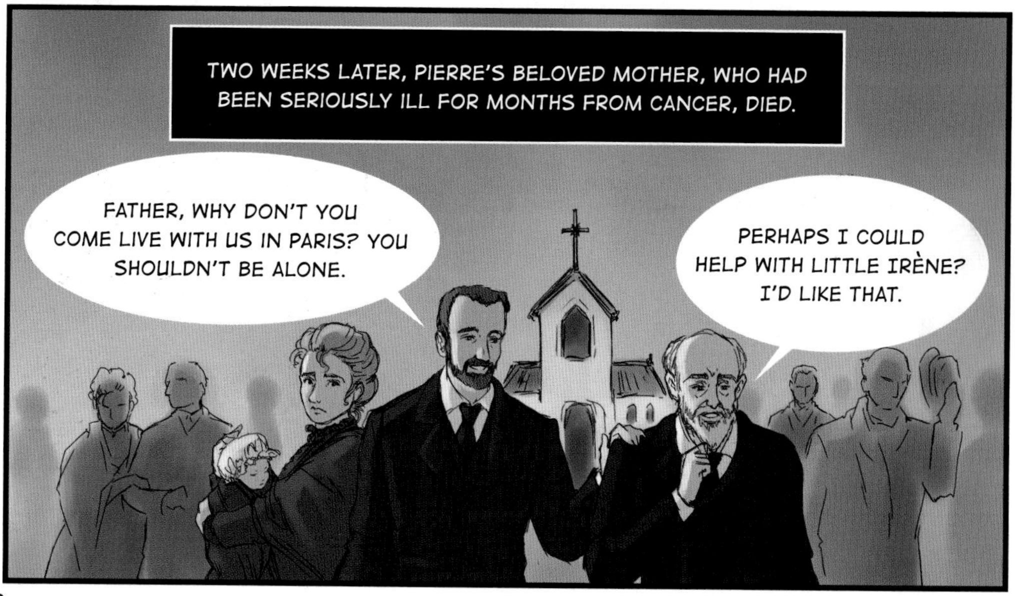
TWO WEEKS LATER, PIERRE'S BELOVED MOTHER, WHO HAD BEEN SERIOUSLY ILL FOR MONTHS FROM CANCER, DIED.
FATHER, WHY DON'T YOU COME LIVE WITH US IN PARIS? YOU SHOULDN'T BE ALONE.
PERHAPS I COULD HELP WITH LITTLE IRÈNE? I'D LIKE THAT.

THE CURIES MOVED TO A SMALL HOUSE WITH A GARDEN ON THE OUTSKIRTS OF PARIS, AND OLD DR. CURIE MOVED IN WITH THEM.

I'M SO GRATEFUL THAT YOU CAN HELP WITH THE BABY. I NEED TIME TO FINISH WRITING UP MY RESEARCH. IT'S GOING TO BE MY FIRST PUBLISHED PAPER.

DR. CURIE HAPPILY TOOK CARE OF IRÈNE...

...WHILE MARIE WORKED IN THE LAB DURING THE DAY.

BUT MARIE ALWAYS MADE SURE TO BE HOME IN TIME TO GIVE IRÈNE HER NIGHTLY BATH.

CHAPTER 6

Mysterious Rays

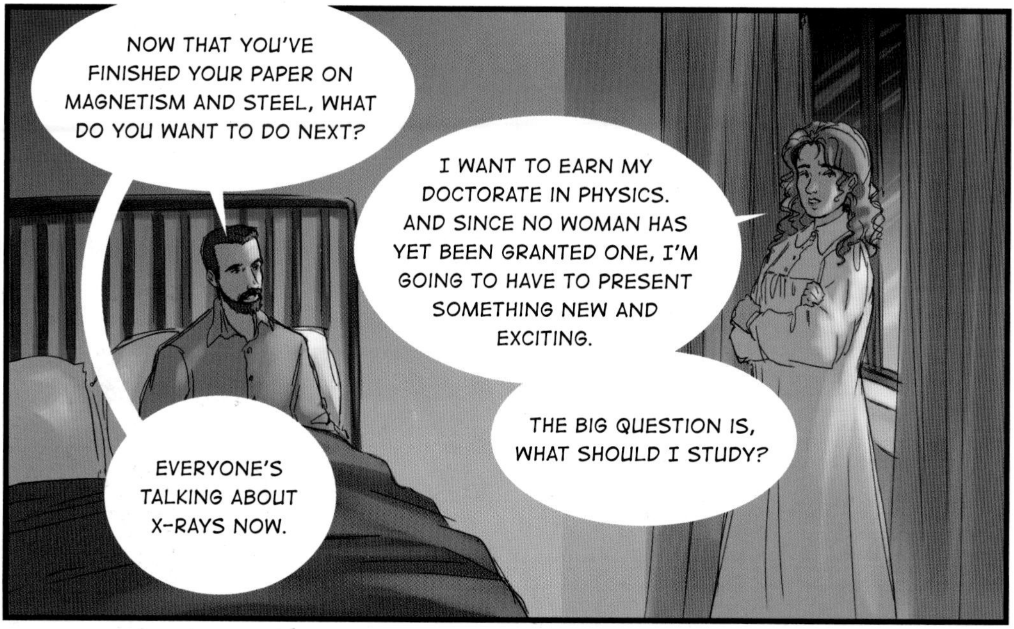
NOW THAT YOU'VE FINISHED YOUR PAPER ON MAGNETISM AND STEEL, WHAT DO YOU WANT TO DO NEXT?
I WANT TO EARN MY DOCTORATE IN PHYSICS. AND SINCE NO WOMAN HAS YET BEEN GRANTED ONE, I'M GOING TO HAVE TO PRESENT SOMETHING NEW AND EXCITING.
THE BIG QUESTION IS, WHAT SHOULD I STUDY?
EVERYONE'S TALKING ABOUT X-RAYS NOW.

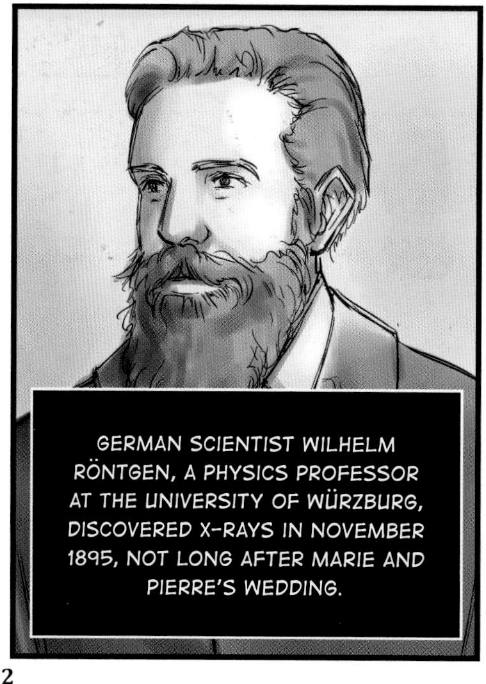
GERMAN SCIENTIST WILHELM RÖNTGEN, A PHYSICS PROFESSOR AT THE UNIVERSITY OF WÜRZBURG, DISCOVERED X-RAYS IN NOVEMBER 1895, NOT LONG AFTER MARIE AND PIERRE'S WEDDING.

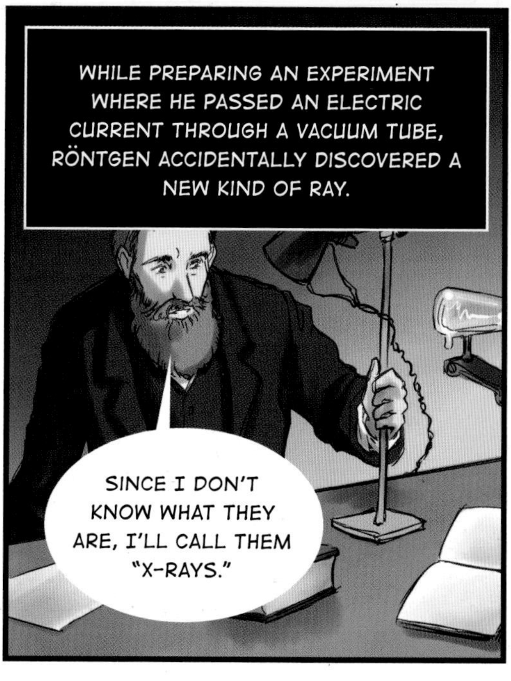
WHILE PREPARING AN EXPERIMENT WHERE HE PASSED AN ELECTRIC CURRENT THROUGH A VACUUM TUBE, RÖNTGEN ACCIDENTALLY DISCOVERED A NEW KIND OF RAY.
SINCE I DON'T KNOW WHAT THEY ARE, I'LL CALL THEM "X-RAYS."

RÖNTGEN IMMEDIATELY STARTED INVESTIGATING THE MYSTERIOUS, INVISIBLE RAYS. HE FOUND THAT X-RAYS COULD "SEE THROUGH" SOLID OBJECTS.

HMMM...THE X-RAYS EASILY PASS THROUGH WOOD, CLOTH, PAPER, AND FLESH, BUT NOT THROUGH DENSER MATERIAL LIKE METAL OR BONE.

THE X-RAYS ALSO AFFECTED PHOTOGRAPHIC PLATES. USING THESE RAYS, HE TOOK AN IMAGE OF HIS WIFE'S HAND THAT SHOWED THE BONES INSIDE.

HOLD STILL, MY DEAR.

I HAVE SEEN MY DEATH!

ON DECEMBER 28, 1895, RÖNTGEN PUBLISHED THE FIRST PAPER ON HIS DISCOVERY: "ON A NEW KIND OF RAY." THE FOLLOWING MONTH, RÖNTGEN DEMONSTRATED HIS FINDINGS AT THE UNIVERSITY OF WÜRZBURG. THE NEWS CAUSED A SENSATION.

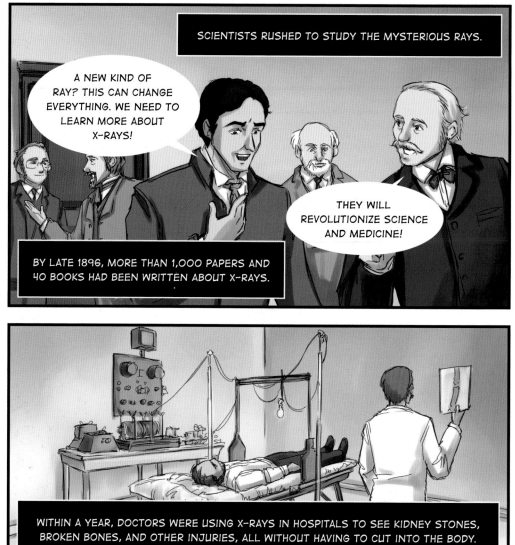

SCIENTISTS RUSHED TO STUDY THE MYSTERIOUS RAYS.

A NEW KIND OF RAY? THIS CAN CHANGE EVERYTHING. WE NEED TO LEARN MORE ABOUT X-RAYS!

THEY WILL REVOLUTIONIZE SCIENCE AND MEDICINE!

BY LATE 1896, MORE THAN 1,000 PAPERS AND 40 BOOKS HAD BEEN WRITTEN ABOUT X-RAYS.

WITHIN A YEAR, DOCTORS WERE USING X-RAYS IN HOSPITALS TO SEE KIDNEY STONES, BROKEN BONES, AND OTHER INJURIES, ALL WITHOUT HAVING TO CUT INTO THE BODY.

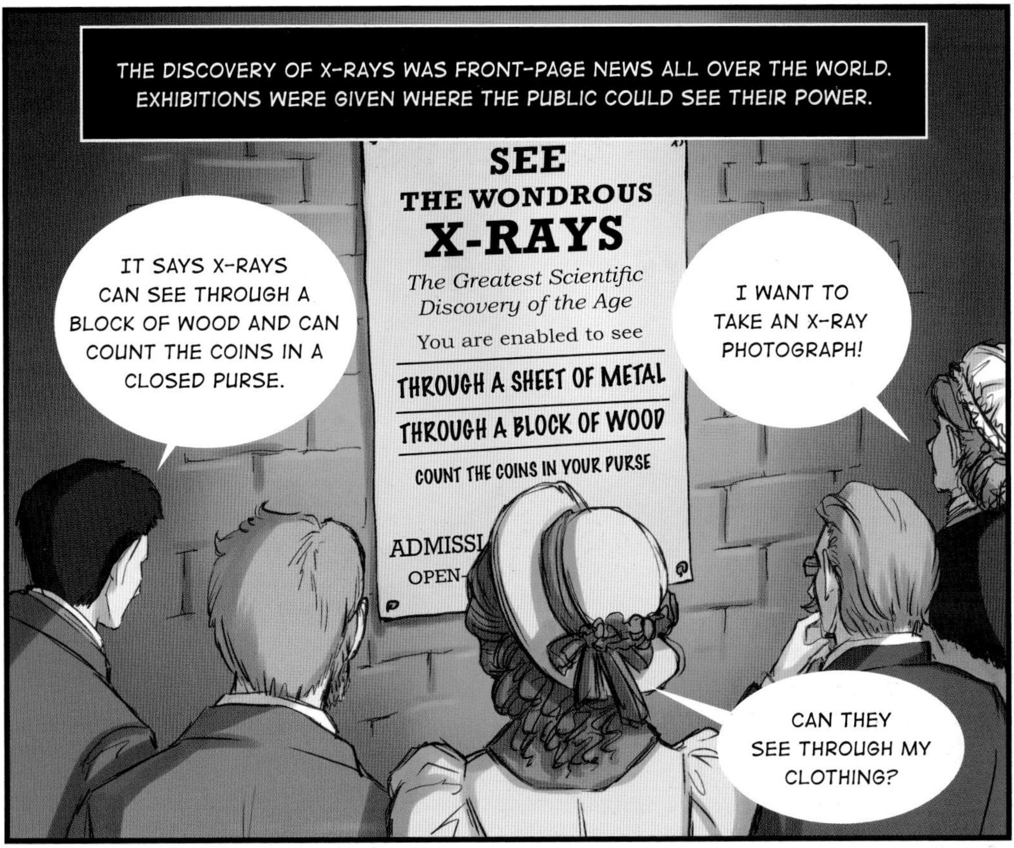
THE DISCOVERY OF X-RAYS WAS FRONT-PAGE NEWS ALL OVER THE WORLD. EXHIBITIONS WERE GIVEN WHERE THE PUBLIC COULD SEE THEIR POWER.
SEE
THE WONDROUS
X-RAYS
The Greatest Scientific Discovery of the Age
You are enabled to see
THROUGH A SHEET OF METAL
THROUGH A BLOCK OF WOOD
COUNT THE COINS IN YOUR PURSE
ADMISSI
OPEN-
IT SAYS X-RAYS CAN SEE THROUGH A BLOCK OF WOOD AND CAN COUNT THE COINS IN A CLOSED PURSE.
I WANT TO TAKE AN X-RAY PHOTOGRAPH!
CAN THEY SEE THROUGH MY CLOTHING?

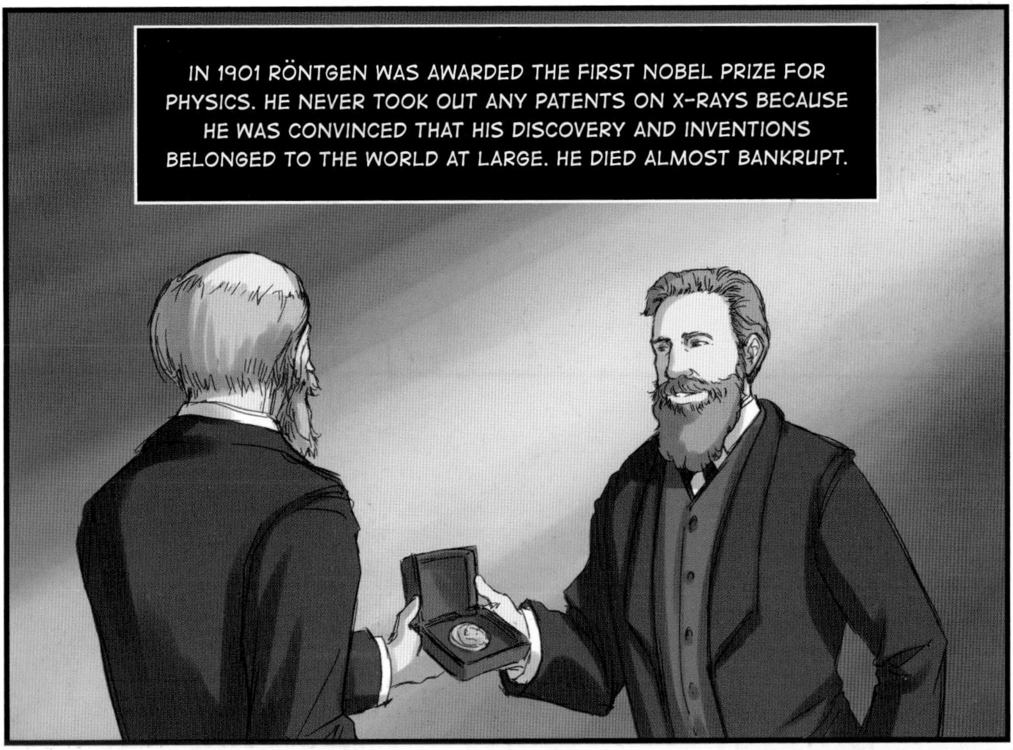
IN 1901 RÖNTGEN WAS AWARDED THE FIRST NOBEL PRIZE FOR PHYSICS. HE NEVER TOOK OUT ANY PATENTS ON X-RAYS BECAUSE HE WAS CONVINCED THAT HIS DISCOVERY AND INVENTIONS BELONGED TO THE WORLD AT LARGE. HE DIED ALMOST BANKRUPT.

THERE ARE STILL MANY QUESTIONS TO BE ANSWERED ABOUT X-RAYS, BUT EVERYONE SEEMS TO BE STUDYING THEM. WHAT ABOUT BECQUEREL'S WORK?

THE PAPERS HE PUBLISHED ON URANIUM RAYS ARE EXCITING.

ANTOINE-HENRI BECQUEREL WAS A FRENCH PHYSICIST FROM A LONG LINE OF DISTINGUISHED SCIENTISTS. HE WAS THE THIRD MEMBER OF HIS FAMILY TO HOLD THE PHYSICS CHAIR AT THE MUSEUM OF NATURAL HISTORY IN PARIS.

THERE'S SO MUCH TO LEARN ABOUT THESE RAYS!

BECQUEREL, LIKE ALMOST ALL THE SCIENTISTS OF THE TIME, WAS FASCINATED BY RÖNTGEN'S DISCOVERY OF X-RAYS.

JUST LIKE HIS FATHER AND GRANDFATHER BEFORE HIM, BECQUEREL WAS INTERESTED IN PHOSPHORESCENCE. PHOSPHORESCENT MATERIALS WOULD GLOW AFTER BEING EXPOSED TO SUNLIGHT.

I WONDER IF PHOSPHORESCENT MATERIALS COULD BE EMITTING X-RAYS AS THEY GLOW?

BECQUEREL HAD PHOSPHORESCENT URANIUM SALTS IN HIS LAB THAT HE COULD USE FOR HIS EXPERIMENT. HE KNEW THAT THESE URANIUM SALT CRYSTALS WOULD GLOW WHEN EXPOSED TO SUNLIGHT.

BECQUEREL PLACED THE URANIUM SALT ON TOP OF A PHOTOGRAPHIC PLATE WRAPPED IN BLACK PAPER AND PUT IT ON A SUNNY WINDOWSILL FOR SEVERAL HOURS. (THE BLACK PAPER WAS USED SO THE SUNLIGHT WOULDN'T AFFECT THE PLATE.)

THE SUNLIGHT WILL MAKE THE SALT GLOW. IF THE GLOWING SALT IS EMITTING X-RAYS, THE RAYS WILL GO THROUGH THE PAPER TO THE PLATE. IF I DEVELOP THE PLATE, I SHOULD GET AN IMAGE JUST LIKE RÖNTGEN DID.

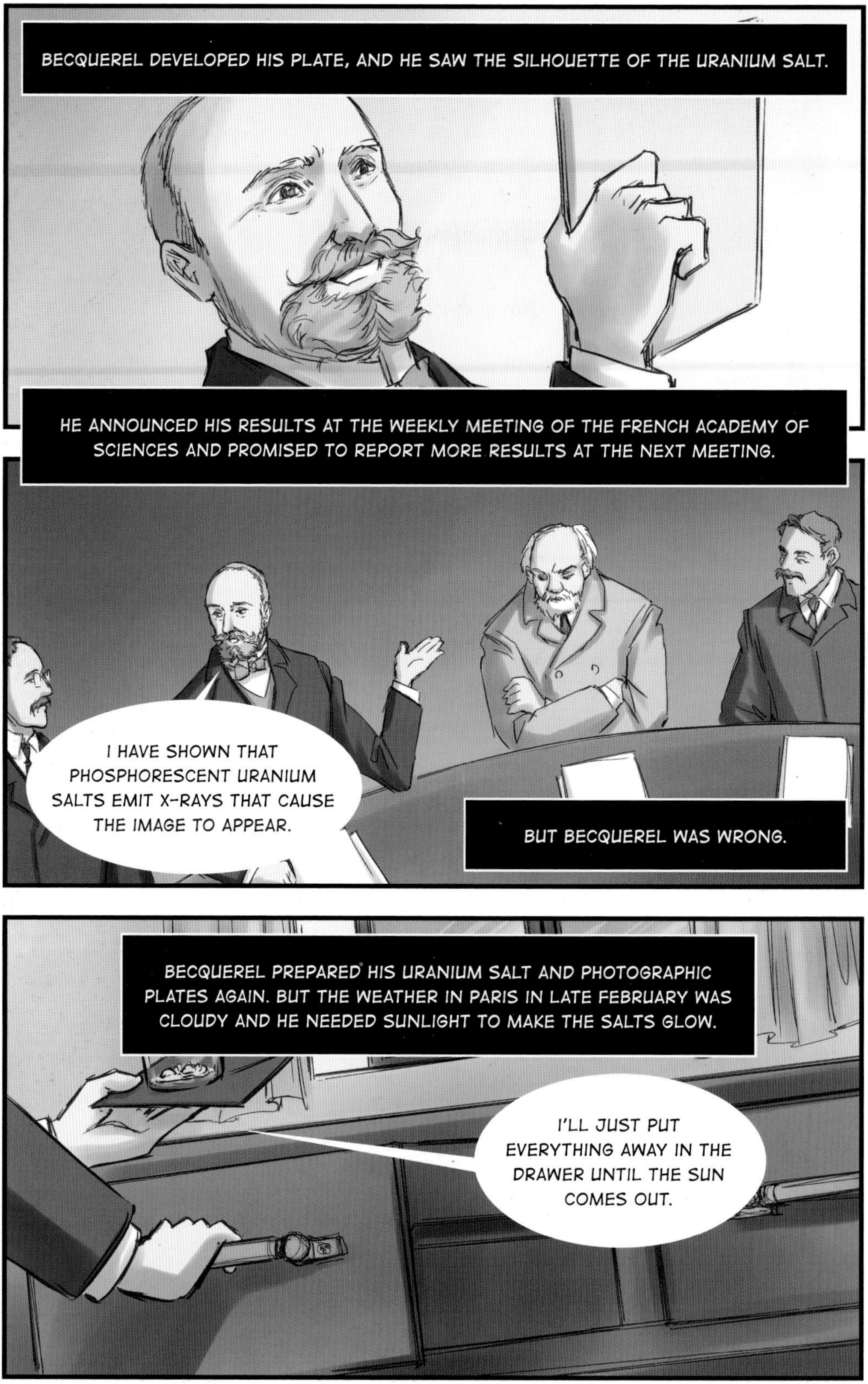
BECQUEREL DEVELOPED HIS PLATE, AND HE SAW THE SILHOUETTE OF THE URANIUM SALT.
HE ANNOUNCED HIS RESULTS AT THE WEEKLY MEETING OF THE FRENCH ACADEMY OF SCIENCES AND PROMISED TO REPORT MORE RESULTS AT THE NEXT MEETING.
I HAVE SHOWN THAT PHOSPHORESCENT URANIUM SALTS EMIT X-RAYS THAT CAUSE THE IMAGE TO APPEAR.
BUT BECQUEREL WAS WRONG.
BECQUEREL PREPARED HIS URANIUM SALT AND PHOTOGRAPHIC PLATES AGAIN. BUT THE WEATHER IN PARIS IN LATE FEBRUARY WAS CLOUDY AND HE NEEDED SUNLIGHT TO MAKE THE SALTS GLOW.
I'LL JUST PUT EVERYTHING AWAY IN THE DRAWER UNTIL THE SUN COMES OUT.

THE NEXT DAY...

CLOUDY AGAIN?

AND THE WEATHER CONTINUED CLOUDY...

I'M GOING TO DEVELOP THE PLATE ANYWAY TO SEE WHAT I GET.

THE IMAGES ARE AS STRONG AND CLEAR AS THE ONES THAT I EXPOSED TO SUNLIGHT!

TO CREATE THE IMAGE, THE URANIUM SALTS MUST HAVE BEEN PRODUCING RAYS ALL ON THEIR OWN IN THE DARK!

BECQUEREL ANNOUNCED HIS NEW FINDINGS.

I AM NOW CONVINCED THAT URANIUM SALTS PRODUCE INVISIBLE RADIATION, EVEN WHEN THEY HAVE BEEN KEPT IN THE DARK.

THEY DO NOT NEED TO BE EXPOSED TO SUNLIGHT TO PRODUCE THIS EFFECT.

BECQUEREL CONTINUED STUDYING THE RAYS FOR THE REST OF THE YEAR AND INTO 1897.

I'VE KEPT THE URANIUM SALTS IN THE DARK FOR SEVERAL MONTHS AND STILL THEY KEEP PRODUCING RAYS!

I'VE TESTED ALL SORTS OF SUBSTANCES THAT CONTAIN THE METAL URANIUM, ONES THAT ARE PHOSPHORESCENT AND ONES THAT AREN'T. THEY ALL GIVE OFF THE MYSTERIOUS RAYS. IT MUST BE THE URANIUM THAT'S GIVING OFF THE RADIATION.

USING AN INSTRUMENT CALLED AN ELECTROSCOPE THAT DETECTS ELECTRICAL CHARGE, HE ALSO SHOWED THAT THE RAYS GIVEN OFF BY URANIUM-CONTAINING SUBSTANCES WERE CAPABLE OF ELECTRIFYING (IONIZING) THE AIR AROUND IT.

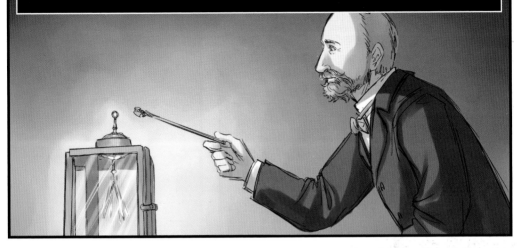

COMPARED TO ALL THE RESEARCH ON X-RAYS, URANIUM RAYS WERE RELATIVELY IGNORED. EVEN BECQUEREL WENT ON TO OTHER TOPICS.

SO WHAT DO YOU THINK OF BECQUEREL'S RAYS?

ARE THEY JUST A WEAK KIND OF X-RAY? THE IMAGES PRODUCED BY THESE URANIUM RAYS AREN'T AS CLEAR AS THOSE PRODUCED BY RÖNTGEN.

THEY JUST DON'T SEEM AS INTERESTING OR USEFUL AS X-RAYS TO ME.

MARIE AND PIERRE, HOWEVER, THOUGHT BECQUEREL'S RAYS WERE VERY INTERESTING.

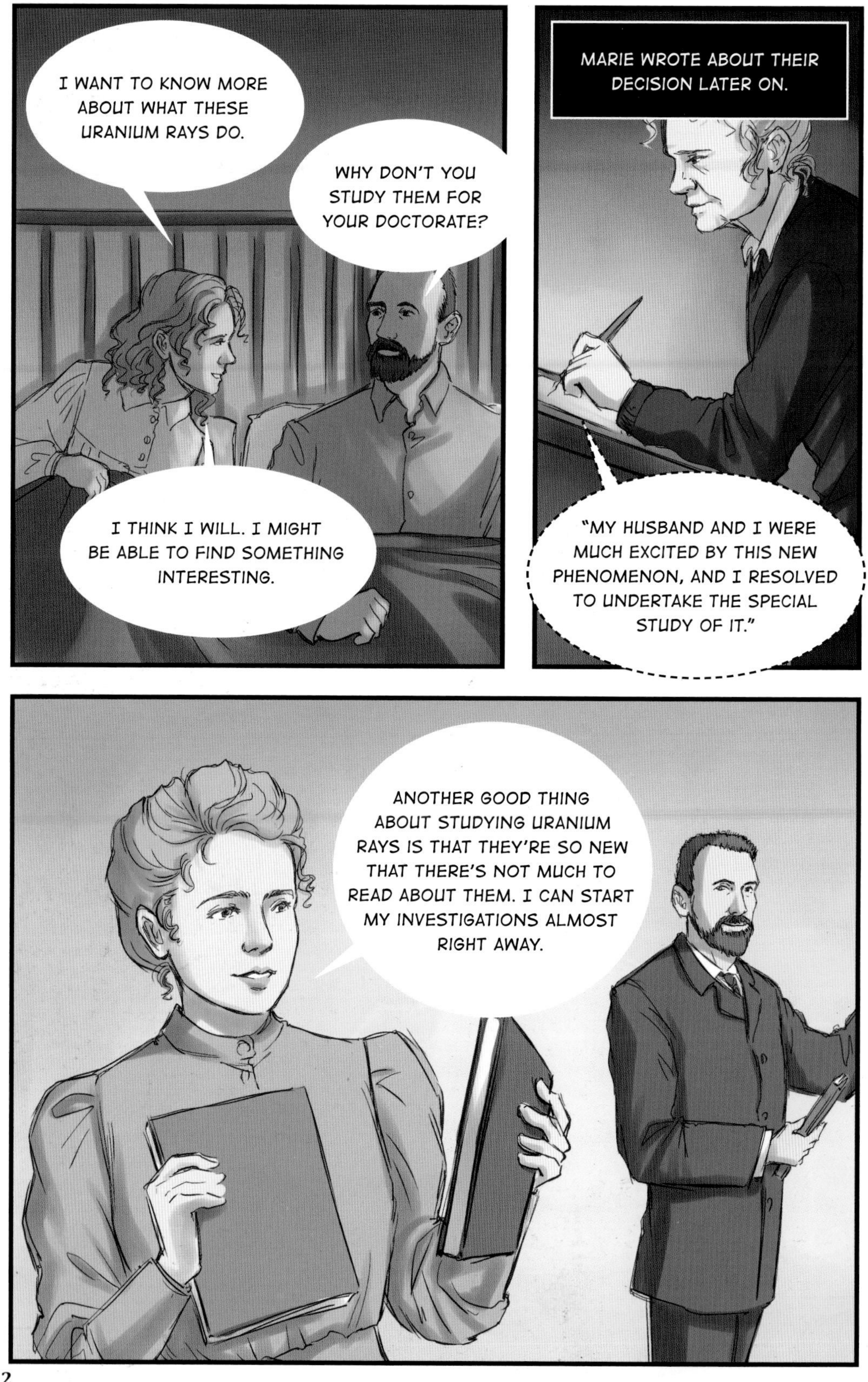
I WANT TO KNOW MORE ABOUT WHAT THESE URANIUM RAYS DO.
WHY DON'T YOU STUDY THEM FOR YOUR DOCTORATE?
I THINK I WILL. I MIGHT BE ABLE TO FIND SOMETHING INTERESTING.
MARIE WROTE ABOUT THEIR DECISION LATER ON.
"MY HUSBAND AND I WERE MUCH EXCITED BY THIS NEW PHENOMENON, AND I RESOLVED TO UNDERTAKE THE SPECIAL STUDY OF IT."
ANOTHER GOOD THING ABOUT STUDYING URANIUM RAYS IS THAT THEY'RE SO NEW THAT THERE'S NOT MUCH TO READ ABOUT THEM. I CAN START MY INVESTIGATIONS ALMOST RIGHT AWAY.

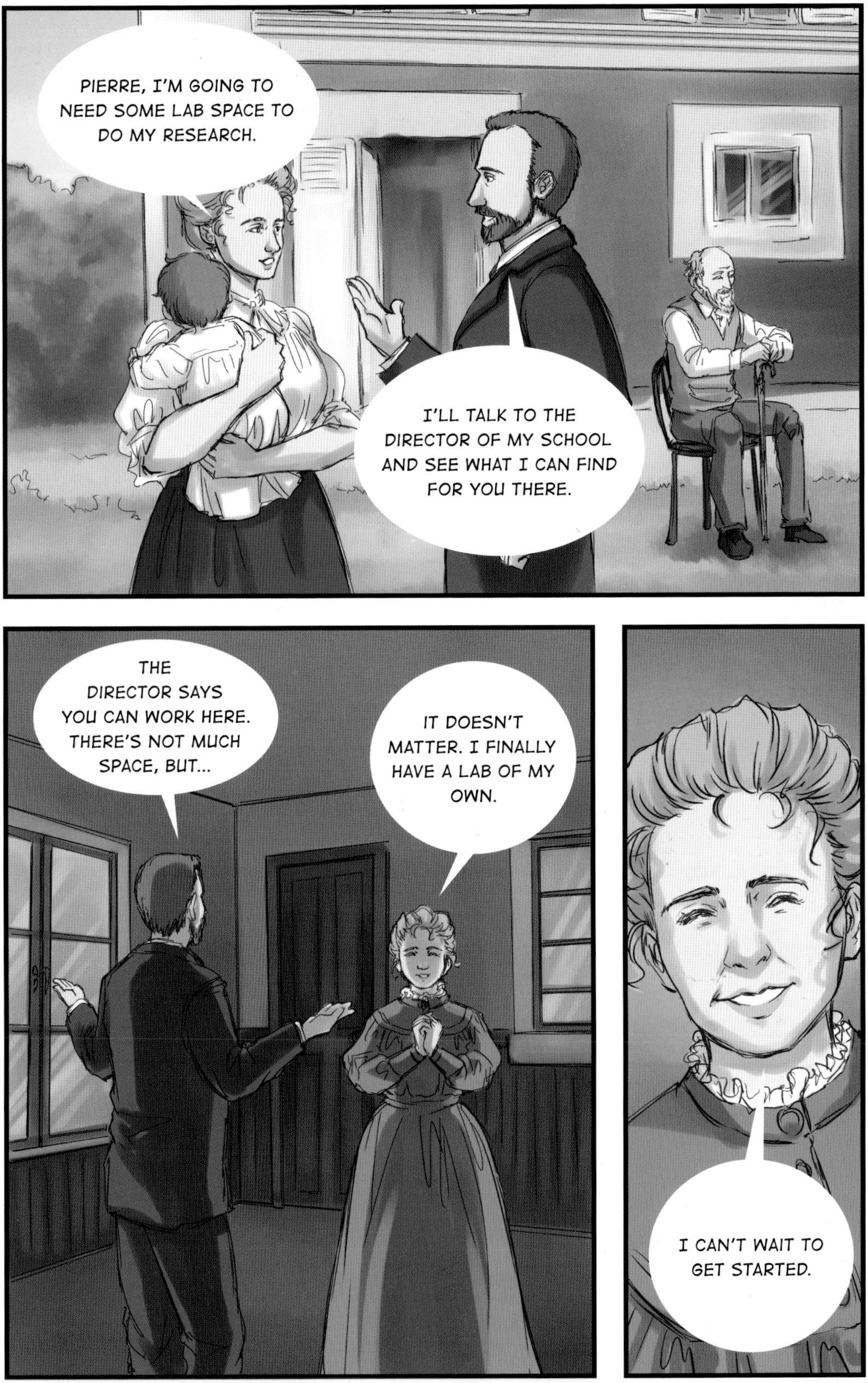
PIERRE, I'M GOING TO NEED SOME LAB SPACE TO DO MY RESEARCH.
I'LL TALK TO THE DIRECTOR OF MY SCHOOL AND SEE WHAT I CAN FIND FOR YOU THERE.
THE DIRECTOR SAYS YOU CAN WORK HERE. THERE'S NOT MUCH SPACE, BUT...
IT DOESN'T MATTER. I FINALLY HAVE A LAB OF MY OWN.
I CAN'T WAIT TO GET STARTED.

MATTER, ATOMS, AND ELEMENTS

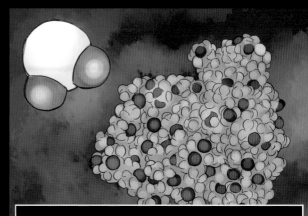

SOME ATOMS COMBINE WITH OTHER ATOMS, STICKING TOGETHER IN GROUPS CALLED MOLECULES. SOME SIMPLE MOLECULES ARE MADE UP OF ONLY TWO ATOMS; OTHERS CAN BE MADE UP OF THOUSANDS.

EVERYTHING THAT EXISTS IN THE UNIVERSE IS MADE OF MATTER, AND ALL MATTER IS MADE UP OF TINY PARTICLES CALLED ATOMS. AT THE TIME THAT MARIE STARTED HER RESEARCH, THE ATOM WAS CONSIDERED TO BE THE SMALLEST PARTICLE OF MATTER.

SOME TYPES OF MATTER ARE MADE UP OF ONLY ONE TYPE OF ATOM. THESE BASIC SUBSTANCES ARE CALLED ELEMENTS. GOLD IS AN ELEMENT, AS ARE CARBON, HYDROGEN, OXYGEN, AND URANIUM. EACH ELEMENT HAS SPECIFIC PHYSICAL AND CHEMICAL PROPERTIES THAT HELP TO IDENTIFY IT.

TWO OR MORE ELEMENTS CAN COMBINE TO FORM SUBSTANCES CALLED COMPOUNDS. THESE COMPOUNDS EACH HAVE A SPECIFIC FORMULA. THE COMPOUND WATER, FOR EXAMPLE, IS MADE UP OF TWO PARTS HYDROGEN AND ONE PART OXYGEN. JUST LIKE ELEMENTS, COMPOUNDS HAVE SPECIFIC PHYSICAL AND CHEMICAL PROPERTIES THAT IDENTIFY THEM.

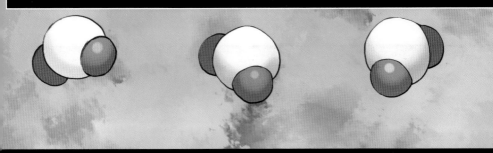

SOME ELEMENTS, SUCH AS GOLD, HAVE BEEN KNOWN FOR THOUSANDS OF YEARS. OTHERS WEREN'T DISCOVERED UNTIL MUCH LATER. AS MORE ELEMENTS WERE DISCOVERED IN THE 1800s, SCIENTISTS WERE DISCOVERING PATTERNS IN HOW THE ELEMENTS BEHAVED.

IN 1869, DMITRI MENDELEEV, A RUSSIAN CHEMIST, ARRANGED THE 63 KNOWN ELEMENTS INTO A TABLE ACCORDING TO THEIR PROPERTIES AND THEIR ATOMIC WEIGHT: WHAT A SINGLE ATOM OF THE ELEMENT WAS BELIEVED TO WEIGH. USING THIS TABLE, MENDELEEV WAS ABLE TO PREDICT THE PROPERTIES OF ELEMENTS THAT WERE STILL UNDISCOVERED.

WHEN MARIE WAS WORKING IN THE 1890s, OVER 70 ELEMENTS HAD ALREADY BEEN DISCOVERED. (TODAY THERE ARE 118.)

CHAPTER 7

GREAT DISCOVERIES

MARIE STARTED HER INVESTIGATIONS IN THE WINTER OF 1897.

I WANT TO STUDY THE POWER OF URANIUM RAYS TO ELECTRIFY THE AIR AROUND THEM, BUT THE EFFECT IS SO SMALL IT'S HARD TO MEASURE.

I THINK THE ELECTROMETER I INVENTED CAN HELP.

PIERRE AND MARIE ADAPTED HIS ELECTROMETER AND USED OTHER LAB EQUIPMENT TO COME UP WITH A WAY TO MEASURE THE TINY ELECTRICAL EFFECTS OF HER SAMPLES.

THIS WILL HELP ME MEASURE THE AMOUNT AND INTENSITY OF THE RADIATION.

MAKING THE MEASUREMENTS WASN'T EASY. HANDLING THE SENSITIVE EQUIPMENT REQUIRED INCREDIBLE DEXTERITY, CONCENTRATION, AND STEADY HANDS.

THE TEMPERATURE AND HUMIDITY IN THIS ROOM CHANGE CONSTANTLY, WHICH MAKES EXACT MEASUREMENTS HARD TO GET. I HAVE TO BE EXTRA CAREFUL, BUT I'M GETTING PRECISE RESULTS THAT CAN BE REPEATED.

MARIE RECORDED EVERYTHING IN HER LAB NOTEBOOKS, INCLUDING THE ROOM TEMPERATURE, WHICH SOMETIMES WENT DOWN TO A CHILLY 43°F (6°C).

BRRR! IT'S FREEZING IN HERE TODAY!

MARIE WAS USED TO WORKING ALONE. WHEN SHE NEEDED DIFFERENT GLASS SHAPES AND TUBES FOR HER EXPERIMENTS, SHE LEARNED HOW TO BLOW GLASS AND MADE THEM HERSELF.

USING THE ELECTROMETER, I CAN SEE THAT BECQUEREL WAS RIGHT. THE AMOUNT OF URANIUM IN THE SAMPLE IS THE SOLE FACTOR IN DETERMINING HOW MUCH RADIATION IS GIVEN OFF.

IT DOESN'T SEEM TO MATTER IF THE URANIUM IS EXPOSED TO HEAT OR LIGHT, IF IT'S WET OR DRY, SOLID OR GROUND TO A POWDER, PURE OR IN A COMPOUND.

IT DOESN'T SEEM TO MATTER HOW THE MOLECULES OF THE COMPOUND ARE ARRANGED OR WHAT OTHER ELEMENTS IT'S MADE UP OF, AS LONG AS THERE'S URANIUM IN IT.

AND, LIKE BECQUEREL, SHE ALSO FOUND THAT THE MORE URANIUM IN A COMPOUND, THE MORE INTENSE THE RADIATION. UNLIKE BECQUEREL, MARIE HAD A REVOLUTIONARY IDEA.

PERHAPS THE ABILITY TO PRODUCE RADIATION HAS NOTHING TO DO WITH THE ARRANGEMENT OF ATOMS IN A MOLECULE. IF THAT'S SO, IT MUST HAVE SOMETHING TO DO WITH THE INTERIOR OF THE ATOM ITSELF.

URANIUM'S ABILITY TO PRODUCE RAYS MUST BE AN ATOMIC PROPERTY THAT EVERY URANIUM ATOM HAS!

THIS IDEA WOULD CONTRIBUTE TO A SHIFT IN THE UNDERSTANDING OF THE ATOM. NOBODY YET GRASPED THE ATOM'S COMPLICATED INNER STRUCTURE OR THE IMMENSE ENERGY WITHIN. THAT WAS STILL TO COME, BUT MARIE'S INSIGHT HELPED OPEN THE DOOR TO THOSE DISCOVERIES.

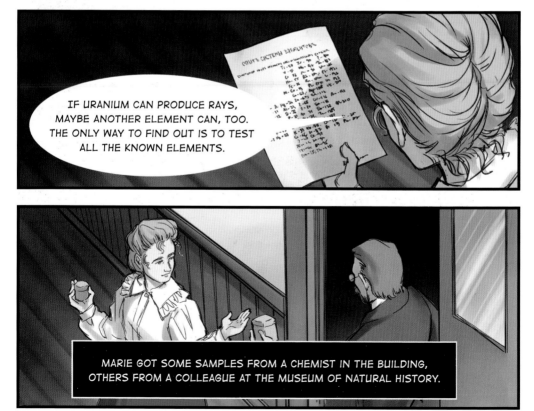

IF URANIUM CAN PRODUCE RAYS, MAYBE ANOTHER ELEMENT CAN, TOO. THE ONLY WAY TO FIND OUT IS TO TEST ALL THE KNOWN ELEMENTS.

MARIE GOT SOME SAMPLES FROM A CHEMIST IN THE BUILDING, OTHERS FROM A COLLEAGUE AT THE MUSEUM OF NATURAL HISTORY.

SINCE THE RAYS WERE NO LONGER JUST FOUND IN URANIUM, THEY COULDN'T BE CALLED URANIUM RAYS ANY LONGER.

"IT WAS NECESSARY AT THIS POINT TO FIND A NEW TERM TO DEFINE THIS NEW PROPERTY OF MATTER MANIFESTED BY THE ELEMENTS OF URANIUM AND THORIUM. I PROPOSED THE WORD RADIOACTIVITY, WHICH HAS SINCE BEEN GENERALLY ADOPTED..."

I'VE TESTED ALL THE KNOWN ELEMENTS AND ONLY URANIUM AND THORIUM WERE RADIOACTIVE. I'M GOING TO TEST COMPOUND MINERALS NEXT.

WELL, AS EXPECTED, MINERALS THAT DON'T CONTAIN ANY URANIUM OR THORIUM DON'T EMIT RAYS.

BUT WHEN SHE STARTED TESTING MINERALS THAT CONTAINED URANIUM, SUCH AS PITCHBLENDE AND CHALCOLITE, MARIE GOT A SURPRISING RESULT. THE MINERALS WERE MORE RADIOACTIVE THAN THEY SHOULD BE, CONSIDERING THE AMOUNT OF URANIUM THEY CONTAINED.

COULD I BE DOING SOMETHING WRONG IN MY EXPERIMENT? THESE NUMBERS MUST BE A MISTAKE. HOW CAN PITCHBLENDE BE THREE OR FOUR TIMES MORE RADIOACTIVE THAN THE URANIUM INSIDE IT?

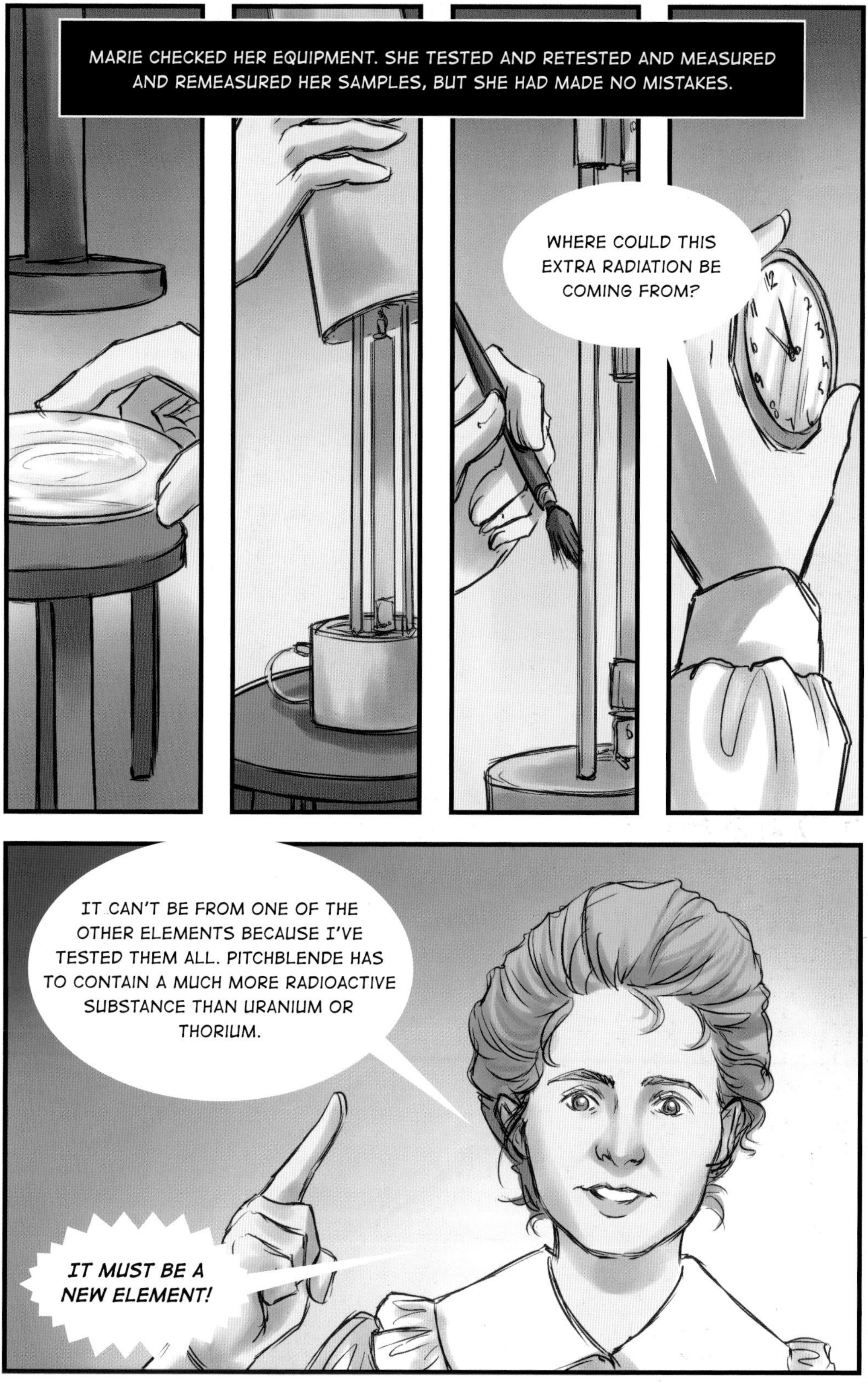
MARIE CHECKED HER EQUIPMENT. SHE TESTED AND RETESTED AND MEASURED AND REMEASURED HER SAMPLES, BUT SHE HAD MADE NO MISTAKES.
WHERE COULD THIS EXTRA RADIATION BE COMING FROM?
IT CAN'T BE FROM ONE OF THE OTHER ELEMENTS BECAUSE I'VE TESTED THEM ALL. PITCHBLENDE HAS TO CONTAIN A MUCH MORE RADIOACTIVE SUBSTANCE THAN URANIUM OR THORIUM.
IT MUST BE A NEW ELEMENT!

MARIE WAS SO EXCITED THAT SHE RUSHED TO BRONIA'S HOUSE TO TELL HER THE NEWS.

THE RADIATION COMES FROM A NEW ELEMENT! I HAVE TO FIND IT!

I KNOW YOU WILL!

MARIE IMMEDIATELY WROTE UP HER RESULTS IN A PAPER TITLED "RAYS EMITTED BY COMPOUNDS OF URANIUM AND OF THORIUM," PUBLISHED ON APRIL 12, 1898.

"TWO MINERALS OF URANIUM, PITCHBLENDE AND CHALCOLITE, ARE MUCH MORE ACTIVE THAN URANIUM ITSELF. THIS FACT IS MOST REMARKABLE, AND SUGGESTS THAT THESE MINERALS MAY CONTAIN AN ELEMENT MUCH MORE ACTIVE THAN URANIUM."

I'M GOING TO GIVE UP MY OWN RESEARCH AND HELP YOU FIND THIS NEW ELEMENT. YOUR WORK IS TOO IMPORTANT.

IF WE JOIN FORCES, WE'LL FIND IT EVEN FASTER!

MARIE WAS NOT ALLOWED TO PRESENT HER RESEARCH TO THE FRENCH ACADEMY OF THE SCIENCES BECAUSE SHE WAS NOT A MEMBER. GABRIEL LIPPMANN PRESENTED IT FOR HER.

WHO IS THIS MARIE SKŁODOWSKA CURIE? A FOREIGNER?

AND A WOMAN!

ISN'T HER HUSBAND PIERRE CURIE? HE'S JUST SOME TEACHER AT A MUNICIPAL SCHOOL.

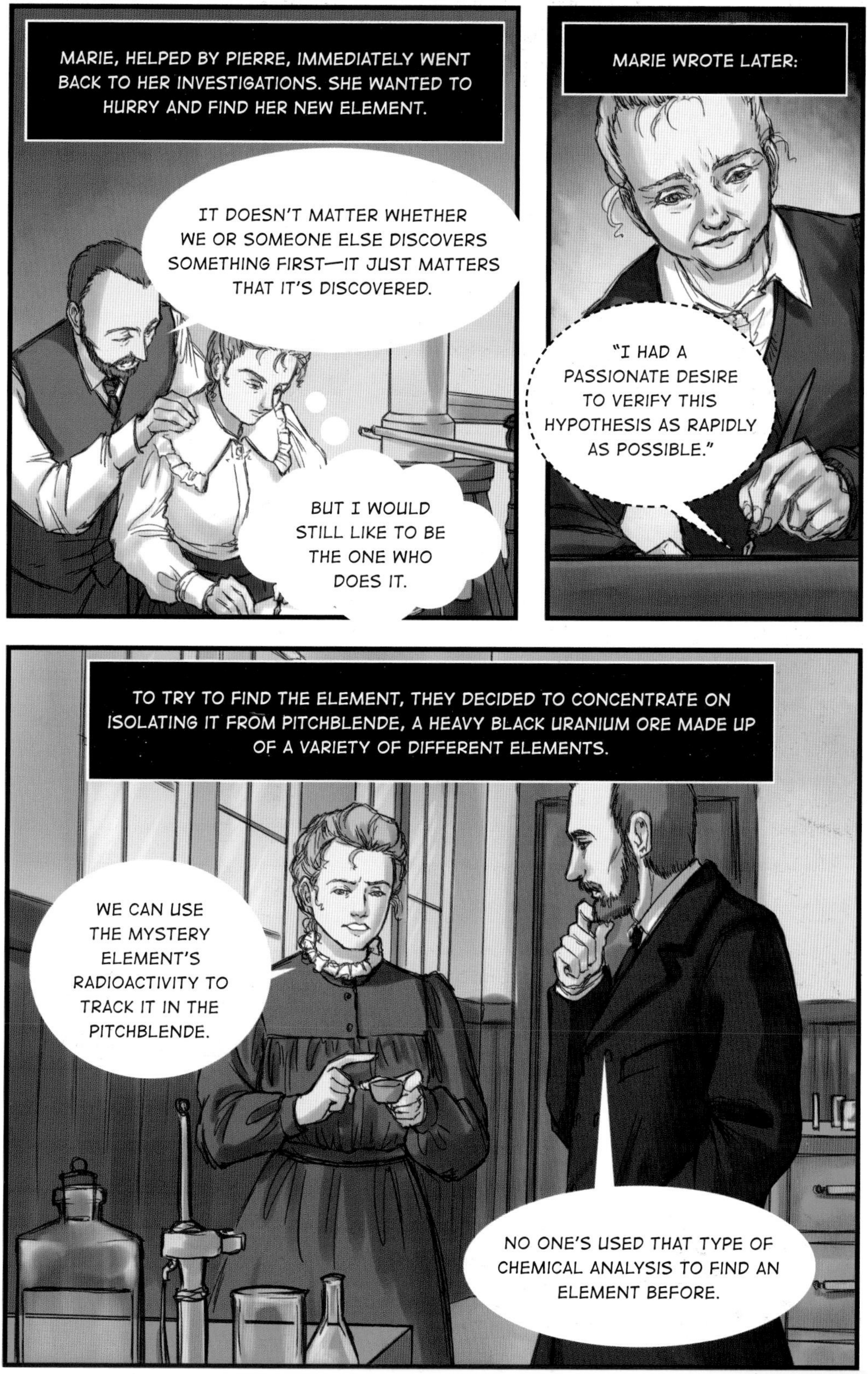
MARIE, HELPED BY PIERRE, IMMEDIATELY WENT BACK TO HER INVESTIGATIONS. SHE WANTED TO HURRY AND FIND HER NEW ELEMENT.
IT DOESN'T MATTER WHETHER WE OR SOMEONE ELSE DISCOVERS SOMETHING FIRST—IT JUST MATTERS THAT IT'S DISCOVERED.
BUT I WOULD STILL LIKE TO BE THE ONE WHO DOES IT.
MARIE WROTE LATER:
"I HAD A PASSIONATE DESIRE TO VERIFY THIS HYPOTHESIS AS RAPIDLY AS POSSIBLE."
TO TRY TO FIND THE ELEMENT, THEY DECIDED TO CONCENTRATE ON ISOLATING IT FROM PITCHBLENDE, A HEAVY BLACK URANIUM ORE MADE UP OF A VARIETY OF DIFFERENT ELEMENTS.
WE CAN USE THE MYSTERY ELEMENT'S RADIOACTIVITY TO TRACK IT IN THE PITCHBLENDE.
NO ONE'S USED THAT TYPE OF CHEMICAL ANALYSIS TO FIND AN ELEMENT BEFORE.

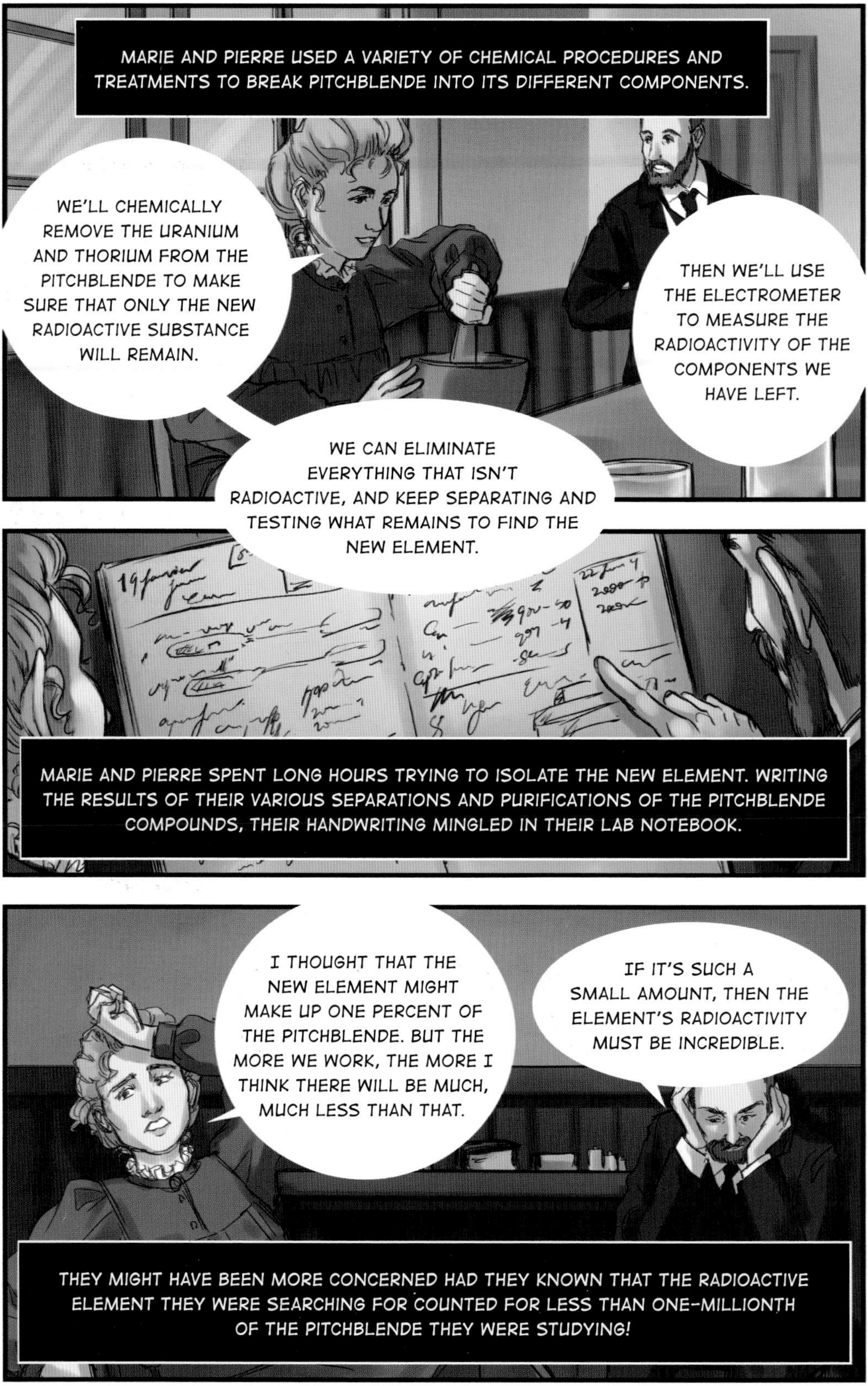
MARIE AND PIERRE USED A VARIETY OF CHEMICAL PROCEDURES AND TREATMENTS TO BREAK PITCHBLENDE INTO ITS DIFFERENT COMPONENTS.
WE'LL CHEMICALLY REMOVE THE URANIUM AND THORIUM FROM THE PITCHBLENDE TO MAKE SURE THAT ONLY THE NEW RADIOACTIVE SUBSTANCE WILL REMAIN.
THEN WE'LL USE THE ELECTROMETER TO MEASURE THE RADIOACTIVITY OF THE COMPONENTS WE HAVE LEFT.
WE CAN ELIMINATE EVERYTHING THAT ISN'T RADIOACTIVE, AND KEEP SEPARATING AND TESTING WHAT REMAINS TO FIND THE NEW ELEMENT.
MARIE AND PIERRE SPENT LONG HOURS TRYING TO ISOLATE THE NEW ELEMENT. WRITING THE RESULTS OF THEIR VARIOUS SEPARATIONS AND PURIFICATIONS OF THE PITCHBLENDE COMPOUNDS, THEIR HANDWRITING MINGLED IN THEIR LAB NOTEBOOK.
I THOUGHT THAT THE NEW ELEMENT MIGHT MAKE UP ONE PERCENT OF THE PITCHBLENDE. BUT THE MORE WE WORK, THE MORE I THINK THERE WILL BE MUCH, MUCH LESS THAN THAT.
IF IT'S SUCH A SMALL AMOUNT, THEN THE ELEMENT'S RADIOACTIVITY MUST BE INCREDIBLE.
THEY MIGHT HAVE BEEN MORE CONCERNED HAD THEY KNOWN THAT THE RADIOACTIVE ELEMENT THEY WERE SEARCHING FOR COUNTED FOR LESS THAN ONE-MILLIONTH OF THE PITCHBLENDE THEY WERE STUDYING!

AS WE KEEP SEPARATING THESE PITCHBLENDE COMPOUNDS, WE'RE GETTING PRODUCTS THAT ARE MORE AND MORE RADIOACTIVE.

THE RADIOACTIVITY SEEMS TO BE CONCENTRATED IN TWO DIFFERENT CHEMICAL BATCHES. ONE CONTAINS THE ELEMENT BISMUTH, AND THE OTHER, THE ELEMENT BARIUM. BOTH ARE EXTREMELY RADIOACTIVE, BUT HAVE DIFFERENT CHEMICAL PROPERTIES.

THE BATCHES MAY ACT LIKE BISMUTH AND BARIUM, BUT NEITHER OF THOSE ELEMENTS ARE RADIOACTIVE.

PIERRE, I BELIEVE WE HAVE FOUND NOT ONE, BUT TWO NEW RADIOACTIVE ELEMENTS IN PITCHBLENDE. LET'S CONCENTRATE ON THE NEW ELEMENT IN THE BISMUTH BATCH FIRST.

BY JULY 1898, THEY WERE CONFIDENT ENOUGH OF THEIR RESULTS TO ANNOUNCE THE DISCOVERY OF THE NEW RADIOACTIVE ELEMENT ASSOCIATED WITH BISMUTH.

YOU WILL HAVE TO NAME IT.

I'D LIKE TO CALL IT POLONIUM TO HONOR MY BELOVED COUNTRY OF POLAND.

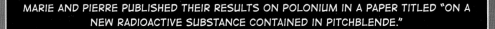

MARIE AND PIERRE PUBLISHED THEIR RESULTS ON POLONIUM IN A PAPER TITLED "ON A NEW RADIOACTIVE SUBSTANCE CONTAINED IN PITCHBLENDE."

DO YOU LIKE THE TITLE?

IT'S TO THE POINT— AND IT WILL BE THE FIRST USE OF THE WORD "RADIOACTIVE."

THEY COULDN'T PRESENT THEIR REPORT AT THE FRENCH ACADEMY OF SCIENCES BECAUSE PIERRE, LIKE MARIE, WASN'T A MEMBER. ON JULY 18, 1898, HENRI BECQUEREL PRESENTED THE RESEARCH FOR THEM. MARIE AND PIERRE WERE HONEST ABOUT THEIR DIFFICULTIES.

"WE HAVE NOT FOUND ANY EXACT PROCEDURE FOR SEPARATING THE ACTIVE SUBSTANCE FROM BISMUTH..."

BUT AT THE SAME TIME THEY HAD OBTAINED A SUBSTANCE THAT WAS 400 TIMES AS ACTIVE AS URANIUM AND HAD FOUND NOTHING LIKE IT AMONG THE KNOWN ELEMENTS.

"WE BELIEVE THEREFORE THAT THE SUBSTANCE THAT WE HAVE REMOVED FROM PITCHBLENDE CONTAINS A METAL NOT YET REPORTED, CLOSE TO BISMUTH IN ITS ANALYTICAL PROPERTIES. IF THE EXISTENCE OF THIS NEW METAL IS CONFIRMED, WE PROPOSE TO CALL IT POLONIUM."

EVEN THOUGH SHE WASN'T A MEMBER, THE FRENCH ACADEMY OF SCIENCES HAD STARTED TO TAKE NOTICE OF MARIE'S WORK. IN JULY 1898, IT AWARDED HER A PRIZE CALLED THE PRIX GEGNER.

MARIE, YOU'VE WON A PRIZE FOR YOUR WORK ON MAGNETISM AND STEEL, AND ON RADIOACTIVITY. IT'S 3,800 FRANCS!

LOOK, IT SAYS: "THE RESEARCH OF MADAME CURIE DESERVES THE ENCOURAGEMENT OF THE ACADEMY."

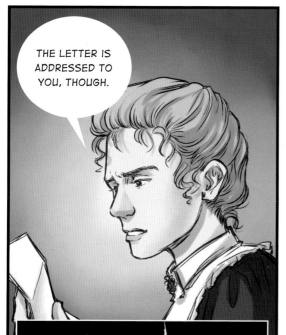

THE LETTER IS ADDRESSED TO YOU, THOUGH.

THOUGH THE ACADEMY MIGHT BE WILLING TO AWARD A PRIZE TO A WOMAN, THEY WEREN'T WILLING TO INFORM HER DIRECTLY.

ALL THAT MATTERS IS THE WORK—AND THE PRIZE MONEY WILL HELP PAY FOR OUR RESEARCH.

AFTER THE PUBLICATION OF THEIR PAPER ON POLONIUM, THE CURIES LEFT PARIS TO VACATION IN THE COUNTRY. THEY SWAM, BICYCLED, AND RESTED, BUT ALSO THOUGHT AND TALKED ABOUT THE NEXT STEP OF THEIR RESEARCH.

MARIE'S OBSESSION WITH HER WORK HAD ONE SAD INTERRUPTION. BRONIA AND HER HUSBAND WERE LEAVING PARIS, RETURNING TO POLAND TO BUILD A TREATMENT CENTER FOR TUBERCULOSIS PATIENTS.

MARIE AND PIERRE WERE SOON BACK AT WORK. AIDED BY GUSTAVÉ BEMONT, A CHEMIST AT THE UNIVERSITY, THEY REFINED THE RADIOACTIVE BATCH ASSOCIATED WITH THE BARIUM.

THIS ELEMENT IS 900 TIMES MORE RADIOACTIVE THAN URANIUM!

I WANT TO PRESENT MORE PROOF THAT IT EXISTS. I WANT SPECTROSCOPIC EVIDENCE, TOO.

SCIENTISTS ALREADY KNEW THAT WHEN AN ELEMENT WAS HEATED TO A GASEOUS STATE AND THE LIGHT IT EMITTED WAS STUDIED THROUGH A PRISM, A SPECIFIC SET OF LINES WAS PRODUCED ALONG THE SPECTRUM OF COLORS. NEW ELEMENTS COULD BE IDENTIFIED IF THEY REVEALED A UNIQUE SET OF SPECTRAL LINES.

WE HAD A SPECTROSCOPY EXPERT TEST THE POLONIUM AND THE EXPERIMENT FAILED.

BUT THE SAMPLE PROBABLY WASN'T PURE ENOUGH. PERHAPS THIS ONE WILL WORK.

MARIE AND PIERRE WENT TO SEE FAMOUS SPECTROSCOPIST EUGÈNE-ANATOLE DEMARÇAY WITH THEIR SAMPLE.

SO YOU'RE BACK! AND WHAT DO YOU HAVE FOR ME TO TEST THIS TIME?

WE THINK WE MIGHT HAVE ANOTHER NEW ELEMENT MIXED IN WITH THE BARIUM.

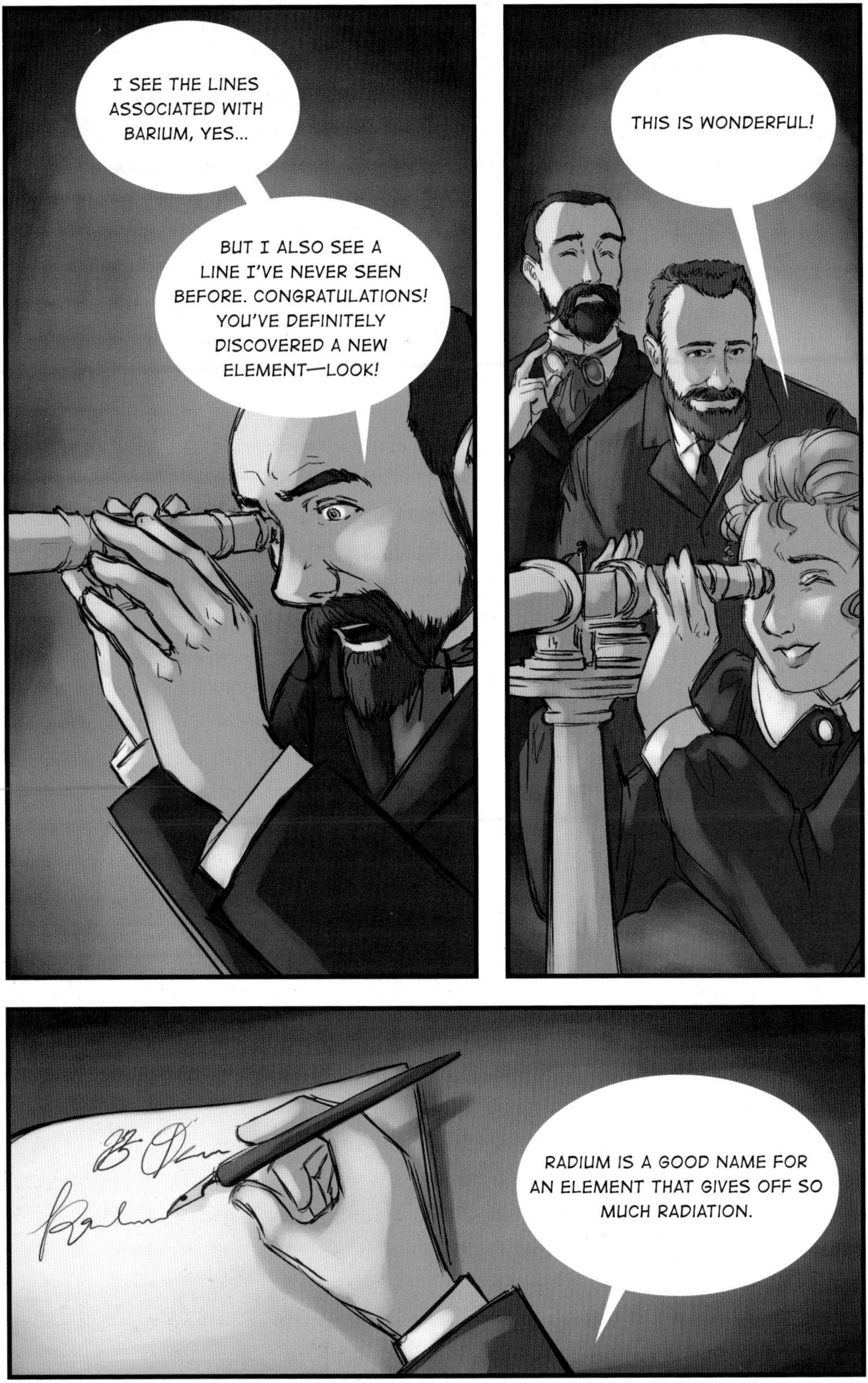
I SEE THE LINES ASSOCIATED WITH BARIUM, YES...
BUT I ALSO SEE A LINE I'VE NEVER SEEN BEFORE. CONGRATULATIONS! YOU'VE DEFINITELY DISCOVERED A NEW ELEMENT—LOOK!
THIS IS WONDERFUL!
RADIUM IS A GOOD NAME FOR AN ELEMENT THAT GIVES OFF SO MUCH RADIATION.

ON DECEMBER 26, 1898, MARIE, PIERRE, AND GUSTAVE BEMONT PUBLISHED A PAPER TITLED "ON A NEW, STRONGLY RADIOACTIVE SUBSTANCE CONTAINED IN PITCHBLENDE."

DEMARÇAY HAS GIVEN US A NOTE TO ADD TO OUR PAPER CONFIRMING THAT HE'S FOUND A NEW SPECTRAL LINE. I HOPE THIS HELPS CONVINCE PEOPLE THAT WE'VE FOUND A NEW ELEMENT.

HENRI BECQUEREL AGAIN PRESENTED MARIE AND PIERRE'S WORK FOR THEM TO THE ACADEMY OF SCIENCES.

"THE VARIOUS REASONS THAT WE HAVE JUST ENUMERATED LEAD US TO BELIEVE THAT THE NEW RADIOACTIVE SUBSTANCE CONTAINS A NEW ELEMENT TO WHICH WE PROPOSE TO GIVE THE NAME RADIUM."

AH, RADIUM—FROM THE LATIN WORD FOR RAY.

DEMARÇAY CONFIRMED THAT HE FOUND A NEW SPECTRAL LINE. THAT ADDS WEIGHT TO THEIR FINDINGS.

BUT FINDING A NEW ELEMENT WITHOUT ACTUALLY ISOLATING IT? JUST BY USING RAYS?

BEFORE I BELIEVE IT, I NEED TO SEE IT. YOU NEED SOMETHING THAT CAN BE SEEN, WEIGHED, AND TOUCHED!

CHAPTER 8

HARD WORK AND SUCCESS

MARIE KNEW THAT SOME SCIENTISTS WOULD NOT BE SATISFIED UNLESS SHE PRODUCED A PURE SAMPLE OF POLONIUM OR RADIUM.

I'M DETERMINED TO PROVIDE PHYSICAL EVIDENCE THAT MY ELEMENTS EXIST.

WE'RE GOING TO NEED A LOT MORE PITCHBLENDE.

GETTING THE PITCHBLENDE POSED A PROBLEM.

THERE'S SO LITTLE POLONIUM AND RADIUM IN PITCHBLENDE THAT WE'RE GOING TO NEED TONS OF IT TO EXTRACT THEM. PITCHBLENDE IS ALSO EXPENSIVE, AND RIGHT NOW WE'RE PAYING FOR EVERYTHING OURSELVES.

PIERRE, WHAT IF WE USED THE RESIDUE THAT'S LEFT AFTER THE URANIUM IS EXTRACTED FROM THE PITCHBLENDE? THE POLONIUM AND RADIUM SHOULD STILL BE THERE.

THE RESIDUE IS BASICALLY A WASTE PRODUCT. IT HAS NO VALUE ONCE THE URANIUM IS GONE. IT SHOULD BE CHEAPER TO GET.

MARIE AND PIERRE FOUND A URANIUM MINE IN BOHEMIA (IN PRESENT-DAY CZECHIA) THAT WAS WILLING TO SEND THEM SEVERAL TONS OF THEIR PITCHBLENDE RESIDUE. THEY WERE JUST DUMPING THE WASTE ROCK IN A NEARBY FOREST. IF MARIE AND PIERRE PAID FOR THE SHIPPING, THEY COULD HAVE IT.

WHERE ARE WE GOING TO PUT IT ALL? WE NEED A BIGGER LAB.

I'LL TALK TO THE DIRECTOR OF MY SCHOOL AGAIN.

IT USED TO BE A DISSECTING ROOM FOR THE MEDICAL SCHOOL, BUT NO ONE'S USED IT FOR A LONG TIME. I'M AFRAID IT'S ALL I HAVE.

WE'LL MAKE THE BEST OF IT.

THE GLASS ROOF LEAKED AND THERE WAS NO LAB EQUIPMENT. IT WAS STIFLINGLY HOT IN THE SUMMER AND FREEZING IN THE WINTER. THERE WERE NO CHIMNEYS TO VENT AWAY HARMFUL FUMES. IT WAS WHERE MARIE AND PIERRE WERE TO DO THEIR MOST IMPORTANT WORK.

IN THE SPRING OF 1899, THE PITCHBLENDE RESIDUE STARTED ARRIVING FROM BOHEMIA.

IT'S FULL OF PINE NEEDLES FROM THE FOREST!

MARIE AND PIERRE WENT TO WORK. MARIE CARRIED OUT THE CHEMICAL SEPARATIONS AND PIERRE WOULD STUDY THE RADIATION OF THE PRODUCTS THEY OBTAINED.

PERHAPS WE SHOULD CONCENTRATE ON ISOLATING RADIUM FIRST. IT LOOKS AS IF THAT MIGHT BE EASIER.

I AGREE.

MARIE WOULD PROCESS UP TO 44 LB (20 KG) OF THE RESIDUE AT A TIME. SHE'D SIFT OUT THE PINE CONES, NEEDLES, AND ANY OTHER DEBRIS, GRIND DOWN WHAT REMAINED, AND PUT IT OVER A FIRE. SHE WOULD THEN START ON A SERIES OF CHEMICAL TREATMENTS THAT SHE'D HAVE TO DO OVER AND OVER AGAIN TO PURIFY IT.

SOMETIMES MARIE WOULD SPEND THE WHOLE DAY MIXING BOILING MATERIALS WITH AN IRON ROD ALMOST AS TALL AS SHE WAS. SHE LIFTED AND CARRIED AND POURED GIANT, HEAVY POTS OF LIQUID.

OTHER DAYS, SHE HAD TO DO THE MOST DELICATE PROCEDURES TO CRYSTALLIZE HER PRODUCT IN ORDER TO CONCENTRATE THE RADIUM. IT WAS PAINSTAKING WORK.

TO NOT INTERRUPT AN EXPERIMENT, MARIE WOULD MAKE LUNCH FOR HERSELF AND PIERRE IN THEIR LAB.

I WONDER WHAT RADIUM WILL LOOK LIKE WHEN WE FIND IT. WHAT FORM DO YOU THINK IT WILL TAKE?

I DON'T KNOW. I SHOULD LIKE IT TO HAVE A VERY BEAUTIFUL COLOR.

"YET IT WAS IN THIS MISERABLE OLD SHED THAT WE PASSED THE BEST AND HAPPIEST YEARS OF OUR LIFE, DEVOTING OUR ENTIRE DAYS TO OUR WORK."

AS MARIE PURIFIED HER PRODUCTS AND THE RADIUM BECAME MORE CONCENTRATED, THE RADIATION BECAME MORE INTENSE AND IT GAVE OFF HEAT. MOST AMAZINGLY, THE PRODUCTS SHE OBTAINED GLOWED.

IT IS BEAUTIFUL.

THE GLOWING TUBES LOOK LIKE FAINT FAIRY LIGHTS.

IN 1900, PARIS HELD AN INTERNATIONAL CONGRESS OF PHYSICS AS PART OF THE PARIS EXPOSITION, WHICH WAS A WORLD'S FAIR. SCIENTISTS FROM ALL OVER THE WORLD ATTENDED. MARIE AND PIERRE PRESENTED A PAPER, "THE NEW RADIOACTIVE SUBSTANCES AND THE RAYS THEY EMIT." IT MADE A HUGE SPLASH.

WHAT IS THE SOURCE OF RADIATION'S STRANGE ENERGY?

IT DEFIES THE LAWS OF PHYSICS! YOU CAN CONVERT ENERGY FROM ONE FORM TO ANOTHER, BUT IT CAN'T BE CREATED OR DESTROYED.

IT'S A MYSTERY THAT NEEDS TO BE SOLVED!

SO MANY SCIENTISTS ARE INTERESTED IN RADIOACTIVITY NOW. I'M HAPPY TO SEND THEM FREE SAMPLES OF OUR RADIOACTIVE MATERIALS TO STUDY.

BECQUEREL WANTS SOME, TOO—HE WANTS TO PICK UP HIS RESEARCH ON RADIOACTIVITY.

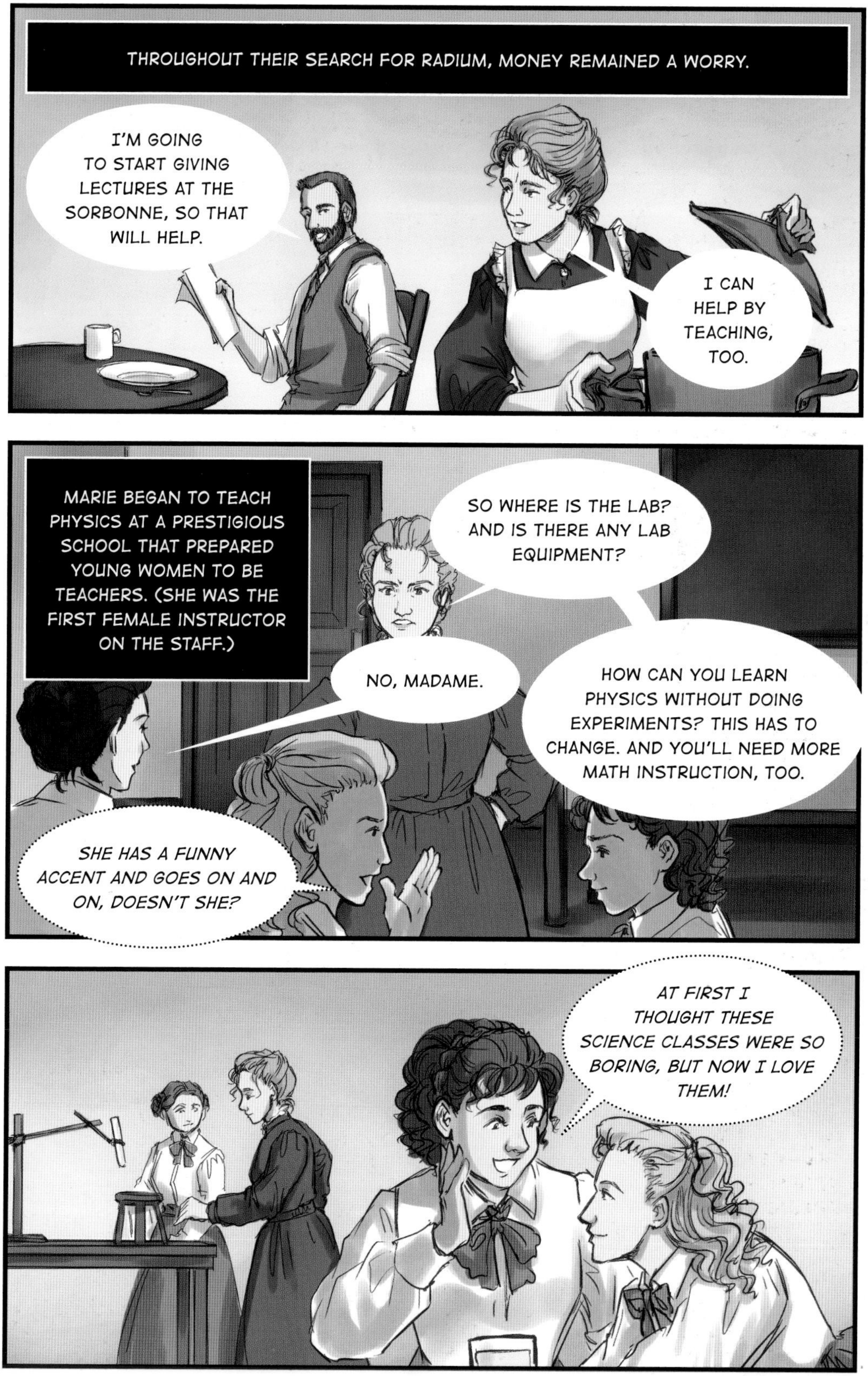
THROUGHOUT THEIR SEARCH FOR RADIUM, MONEY REMAINED A WORRY.
I'M GOING TO START GIVING LECTURES AT THE SORBONNE, SO THAT WILL HELP.
I CAN HELP BY TEACHING, TOO.
MARIE BEGAN TO TEACH PHYSICS AT A PRESTIGIOUS SCHOOL THAT PREPARED YOUNG WOMEN TO BE TEACHERS. (SHE WAS THE FIRST FEMALE INSTRUCTOR ON THE STAFF.)
SO WHERE IS THE LAB? AND IS THERE ANY LAB EQUIPMENT?
NO, MADAME.
HOW CAN YOU LEARN PHYSICS WITHOUT DOING EXPERIMENTS? THIS HAS TO CHANGE. AND YOU'LL NEED MORE MATH INSTRUCTION, TOO.
SHE HAS A FUNNY ACCENT AND GOES ON AND ON, DOESN'T SHE?
AT FIRST I THOUGHT THESE SCIENCE CLASSES WERE SO BORING, BUT NOW I LOVE THEM!

IN 1902, AFTER ALMOST FOUR YEARS OF WORK, AND GOING THROUGH THOUSANDS OF CRYSTALLIZATIONS FROM SEVERAL TONS OF PITCHBLENDE RESIDUE, MARIE FINALLY HAD A TENTH OF A GRAM OF RADIUM CHLORIDE, ABOUT THE SIZE OF A GRAIN OF RICE. FROM THIS SHE WAS ALSO ABLE TO MAKE A FIRST DETERMINATION OF RADIUM'S ATOMIC WEIGHT.

WE FINALLY HAVE PHYSICAL EVIDENCE, PIERRE! RADIUM OFFICIALLY EXISTS!

AS MARIE AND PIERRE WORKED ON ISOLATING RADIUM AND STUDYING ITS EFFECTS, THEY WROTE DOZENS OF SCIENTIFIC PAPERS, ALONE, TOGETHER, AND WITH OTHER SCIENTISTS, REVEALING THEIR DISCOVERIES AS THEY HAPPENED. MARIE ALSO PREPARED THE TEXT OF THE WORK SHE WAS GOING TO SUBMIT FOR HER DOCTORATE IN SCIENCE AT THE SORBONNE.

BRONIA HAD COME ALL THE WAY TO PARIS TO SEE HER LITTLE SISTER GIVE HER DOCTORAL PRESENTATION AT THE SORBONNE.

YOU NEED A NEW DRESS. NO COMPLAINING—THIS IS A BIG OCCASION!

I AM SO GLAD THAT BRONIA IS HERE. SHE ALWAYS KNOWS WHAT TO DO.

MARIE PRESENTED HER RESEARCH ON RADIOACTIVITY AND HER DISCOVERY OF RADIUM FOR HER DOCTORAL THESIS AT THE SORBONNE ON JUNE 25, 1903. MARIE HAD TO ANSWER QUESTIONS ABOUT HER WORK AND EXPLAIN WHAT SHE ACCOMPLISHED.

YOUR FINDINGS REPRESENT THE GREATEST SCIENTIFIC CONTRIBUTION EVER MADE IN A DOCTORAL THESIS.

THE UNIVERSITY ACCORDS YOU THE TITLE OF DOCTOR OF PHYSICAL SCIENCE. AND IN THE NAME OF THE JURY, MADAME, I WISH TO EXPRESS TO YOU ALL OUR CONGRATULATIONS.

SHE'S SUCH AN ENCOURAGEMENT TO OTHER WOMEN! I'M SO PROUD SHE'S OUR TEACHER.

MARIE BECAME THE FIRST WOMAN IN FRANCE TO BE AWARDED A DOCTORATE IN SCIENCE.

CONGRATULATIONS, MARIE!

PIERRE TOASTED MARIE WITH A GLOWING TUBE OF RADIUM SALTS, BUT BY ITS LIGHT, IT WAS CLEAR THAT HIS FINGERS WERE SCARRED AND CRACKED.

MARIE AND PIERRE DIDN'T KNOW IT, BUT THEY WERE STARTING TO BE AFFECTED BY THEIR EXPOSURE TO RADIOACTIVE MATERIALS. AT THE TIME, NO ONE KNEW EXACTLY HOW DANGEROUS RADIOACTIVITY WAS—IT WAS A COMPLETELY NEW PHENOMENON.

MY LEGS AND ARMS ACHE SO MUCH. I ALWAYS FEEL TIRED AND ILL NOW.

IT'S JUST BECAUSE YOU'RE WORKING SO HARD, AT SCHOOL AND IN THE LAB.

I'VE LOST ALMOST 10 POUNDS SINCE I'VE STARTED WORKING ON RADIUM. I'M ALSO VERY TIRED, BUT I THINK WE JUST NEED MORE REST.

MARIE AND PIERRE ALREADY KNEW THAT RADIOACTIVE MATERIALS CAUSED BURNS. BECQUEREL HAD PLACED RADIOACTIVE MATERIAL AGAINST HIS ARM AND STUDIED THE BURN, WOUND, AND EVENTUAL SCAR IT MADE. PIERRE AND BECQUEREL HAD WRITTEN A PAPER ON THE EFFECT, BUT THEY ALL TENDED TO MAKE LIGHT OF THEIR INJURIES.

I'M DELIGHTED AND ANNOYED THAT MY TUBE OF RADIUM HAS BURNED MY SKIN. I LOVE IT, BUT I HOLD A GRUDGE AGAINST IT!

MY HANDS ARE SCARRED AND BURNED, TOO. IT'S THE PRICE ONE PAYS FOR SCIENCE.

IF RADIUM CAN KILL HEALTHY TISSUE, CAN IT KILL DISEASED TISSUE, TOO?

PIERRE COLLABORATED WITH TWO WELL-KNOWN PROFESSORS OF MEDICINE TO SEE IF RADIUM COULD BE USED TO TREAT DISEASE.

THE RADIUM DESTROYS DISEASED CELLS!

THAT MEANS IT CAN BE USED TO TREAT TUMORS AND OTHER FORMS OF CANCER.

RADIUM IS GOING TO BE VERY USEFUL— AND VERY VALUABLE.

WE HAVE TWO CHOICES. WE CAN LET EVERYONE KNOW ALL OUR RESEARCH AND OUR PROCESS FOR OBTAINING RADIUM FOR FREE OR WE CAN PATENT IT.

PATENTING KNOWLEDGE WOULD BE CONTRARY TO THE SCIENTIFIC SPIRIT.

I AGREE, BUT OUR LIFE IS HARD. THIS PATENT COULD REPRESENT A FORTUNE.

IF RADIUM IS GOING TO BE OF USE IN TREATING DISEASE... IT SEEMS TO ME IMPOSSIBLE TO TAKE ADVANTAGE OF THAT.

I THINK SO, TOO.

CHAPTER 9

FAME AND HEARTBREAK

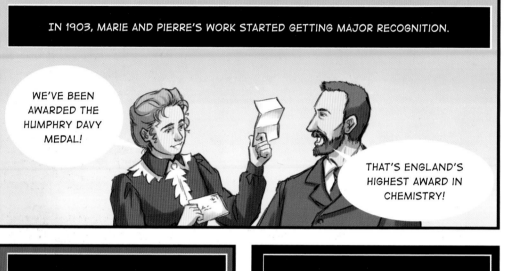

IN 1903, MARIE AND PIERRE'S WORK STARTED GETTING MAJOR RECOGNITION.

WE'VE BEEN AWARDED THE HUMPHRY DAVY MEDAL!

THAT'S ENGLAND'S HIGHEST AWARD IN CHEMISTRY!

LATE THAT YEAR, PIERRE FOUND OUT THAT ONLY HE AND BECQUEREL WERE NOMINATED FOR THE NOBEL PRIZE IN PHYSICS.

HOW COULD A WOMAN BE RESPONSIBLE FOR SUCH REMARKABLE RESEARCH INTO RADIOACTIVITY?

SHE MUST ONLY HAVE BEEN PIERRE CURIE'S ASSISTANT.

PIERRE WROTE TO SUPPORTERS EXPLAINING AND DEFENDING MARIE'S ROLE IN THEIR WORK AND STATED:

"IF IT IS TRUE THAT ONE IS SERIOUSLY THINKING ABOUT ME (FOR THE PRIZE), I WISH TO BE CONSIDERED TOGETHER WITH MADAME CURIE..."

IN THE END, HENRI BECQUEREL AND MARIE AND PIERRE CURIE WERE AWARDED THE 1903 NOBEL PRIZE FOR "THEIR JOINT RESEARCHES ON THE RADIATION PHENOMENA."

MARIE WAS THE FIRST WOMAN TO WIN A NOBEL PRIZE, WHICH ALSO CAME WITH AN AWARD OF 70,000 FRANCS.

WITH THIS MONEY, YOU CAN FINALLY STOP TEACHING AT THE MUNICIPAL SCHOOL. YOU WORK TOO HARD, PIERRE, AND I WORRY ABOUT YOUR HEALTH. I WANT TO GIVE SOME GIFTS TO SOME POLISH STUDENTS, AND I'D LIKE TO SEND MONEY TO BRONIA FOR HER TREATMENT CENTER...

AND NOTHING FOR YOU?

PERHAPS WE CAN INSTALL A MODERN BATHROOM?

AS WINNERS OF THE NOBEL PRIZE, PIERRE AND MARIE WERE TO TRAVEL TO SWEDEN TO ACCEPT A GOLD MEDAL AND GIVE A SPEECH ABOUT THEIR RESEARCH. PIERRE, HOWEVER, WROTE TO THE PRIZE COMMITTEE THAT THEY COULDN'T COME—AT LEAST NOT YET. MARIE HAD SUFFERED A MISCARRIAGE IN THE SUMMER, AND PIERRE HIMSELF, THOUGH HE SAID HE COULDN'T INTERRUPT HIS TEACHING DUTIES, WAS ALSO NOT FEELING WELL.

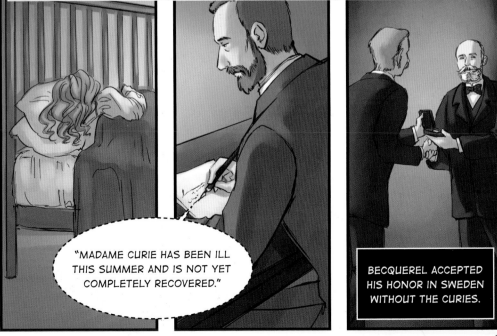

"MADAME CURIE HAS BEEN ILL THIS SUMMER AND IS NOT YET COMPLETELY RECOVERED."

BECQUEREL ACCEPTED HIS HONOR IN SWEDEN WITHOUT THE CURIES.

UPON WINNING THE NOBEL PRIZE, THE CURIES BECAME CELEBRITIES OVERNIGHT. THE PRESS LOVED THE STORY OF THE POOR HUSBAND-AND-WIFE SCIENTIST TEAM.

DID YOU SEE THEIR LAB? IT'S AMAZING THAT THEY WERE ABLE TO WORK THERE!

AND A WOMAN SCIENTIST! HOW STRANGE!

I HATE THIS DISRUPTION OF OUR WORK.

THE MONEY IS WELCOME, BUT I DIDN'T REALIZE THAT WE'D BE SO HOUNDED BY THE PRESS. DID YOU KNOW THAT THEY'RE PERFORMING SKITS OF OUR LIVES IN THEATERS?

SOME AMERICAN JUST WROTE TO ASK IF HE COULD NAME HIS RACEHORSE AFTER ME.

EVERYONE WANTS PHOTOS AND AUTOGRAPHS AND INTERVIEWS.

THIS IS THE DISASTER OF OUR LIVES.

RADIUM CRAZY

MARIE AND PIERRE BECAME FAMOUS, BUT SO DID THEIR DISCOVERY. RADIUM WAS TOUTED AS A WONDER DRUG THAT COULD CURE ALL ILLS, INCLUDING BLINDNESS AND WARTS. ONCE RADIUM STARTED BEING MANUFACTURED COMMERCIALLY, IT WAS ADDED TO EVERYTHING FROM TOOTHPASTE TO HAIR TONICS. SINCE IT GLOWED IN THE DARK, RADIUM WAS USED FOR CHRISTMAS TREE DECORATIONS AND MIXED IN PAINT THAT WAS USED FOR LUMINOUS WATCH AND CLOCK DIALS. THESE PRODUCTS WERE ALL DANGEROUS.

IN THE 1920s, THE GIRLS WHO PAINTED THE WATCH DIALS WERE TAUGHT TO USE THEIR MOUTHS TO MAKE THE TINY PAINTBRUSHES HAVE A FINER POINT. BUT BY DOING THIS, THEY WERE EATING SMALL AMOUNTS OF THE PAINT. THE GIRLS DIDN'T KNOW THE DANGERS OF RADIUM UNTIL THEIR JAWS STARTED DISINTEGRATING AND THEY DEVELOPED CANCER. BUT MARIE AND PIERRE DIDN'T KNOW THAT YET...

AT THE SAME TIME, THERE WERE DEFINITE BENEFITS TO THEIR FAME. A SPECIAL PROFESSORSHIP IN GENERAL PHYSICS WAS CREATED AT THE SORBONNE JUST FOR PIERRE, AND THEY PROMISED TO BUILD HIM A REAL LABORATORY.

I AM LOOKING FORWARD TO HAVING A DECENT LAB TO WORK IN AFTER ALL THESE YEARS.

AND FOR THE FIRST TIME IN MY CAREER, I'LL HAVE A TITLE—CHIEF OF LABORATORY—AND A SALARY.

SO YOU'VE FINALLY BEEN ELECTED TO THE ACADEMY OF SCIENCES? IT'S A GREAT HONOR!

THEY DIDN'T ELECT ME WHEN I TRIED TO BECOME A MEMBER A FEW YEARS AGO. I DON'T KNOW HOW IMPORTANT THESE HONORS REALLY ARE. I JUST CARE ABOUT THE WORK.

AND AFTER HER HEARTBREAKING MISCARRIAGE IN 1903, MARIE BECAME HEALTHY ENOUGH TO GIVE BIRTH TO A BABY GIRL ON DECEMBER 6, 1904.

SHE'S SO CHUBBY! I ADORE MY LITTLE ÈVE DENISE, BUT THAT DOESN'T PREVENT ME FROM ALSO LOVING MY BIG SEVEN-YEAR-OLD DAUGHTER!

RADIOACTIVITY

MARIE AND PIERRE KNEW THAT THERE WAS SOMETHING STRANGE ABOUT RADIUM'S ABILITY TO RELEASE ENERGY. THERE ALSO SEEMED TO BE A LOT OF ENERGY. PIERRE HAD RUN AN EXPERIMENT AND FOUND THAT IT TOOK ONLY ONE HOUR FOR ONE GRAM OF RADIUM TO HEAT ONE GRAM OF WATER FROM FREEZING TO BOILING.

MARIE THOUGHT THAT SOMETHING WAS HAPPENING INSIDE THE ATOM TO CREATE SUCH EFFECTS AND SHE WAS RIGHT. SCIENTIST ERNEST RUTHERFORD WORKED TO EXPLAIN THE PROCESS OF RADIOACTIVITY USING MATERIALS SUPPLIED BY MARIE.

HE THOUGHT THAT RADIOACTIVE ELEMENTS LIKE RADIUM WERE UNSTABLE. AS THE ATOMS WERE SPONTANEOUSLY DISINTEGRATING, THEY WERE DECAYING (CHANGING) INTO OTHER ELEMENTS. RADIOACTIVITY WAS THE ENERGY THAT WAS RELEASED AS THE ATOMS WERE BREAKING APART TO GET TO A MORE STABLE STATE.

THE IDEA THAT ONE ELEMENT COULD CHANGE INTO ANOTHER SEEMED DISTURBING, BUT EVENTUALLY THE CURIES ACCEPTED IT.

IN JUNE 1905, MARIE AND PIERRE FINALLY CAME TO SWEDEN, WHERE PIERRE WOULD DELIVER THE LECTURE REQUIRED OF ALL NOBEL PRIZE WINNERS. HE WAS VERY CAREFUL TO GIVE MARIE THE CREDIT THAT SHE DESERVED. HE ENDED HIS SPEECH WITH A WARNING.

ONE MAY ALSO IMAGINE THAT IN CRIMINAL HANDS RADIUM MIGHT BECOME VERY DANGEROUS, AND HERE WE MAY ASK OURSELVES IF HUMANITY HAS ANYTHING TO GAIN BY LEARNING THE SECRETS OF NATURE...

...POWERFUL EXPLOSIVES HAVE PERMITTED MEN TO PERFORM ADMIRABLE WORK. THEY ARE ALSO A TERRIBLE MEANS OF DESTRUCTION IN THE HANDS OF THE GREAT CRIMINALS WHO LEAD THE PEOPLE TOWARD WAR.

I AM ONE OF THOSE WHO THINK THAT HUMANITY WILL OBTAIN MORE GOOD THAN EVIL FROM THE NEW DISCOVERIES.

THOUGH THEIR LIVES WOULD NEVER GO BACK TO NORMAL AFTER THEIR FAMOUS DISCOVERIES, THEY ADAPTED AND CONTINUED TO WORK. IN APRIL 1906, THEY GAVE THEMSELVES A VACATION IN THE COUNTRYSIDE WITH THEIR CHILDREN.

LIFE HAS BEEN SWEET WITH YOU, MARIE.

ON APRIL 19, 1906, PIERRE RETURNED TO PARIS. HE HAD A BUSY DAY OF MEETINGS AND APPOINTMENTS.

AS HE WAS HURRYING TO CROSS THE STREET, PIERRE WAS STRUCK FROM BEHIND BY A HORSE-DRAWN CART.

THE HORSES REARED AND PIERRE FELL.

HIS SKULL WAS CRUSHED UNDER THE WHEELS, KILLING HIM INSTANTLY.

CHAPTER 10

ANOTHER NOBEL PRIZE AND SCANDAL

EVERYTHING IS OVER, PIERRE IS SLEEPING HIS LAST SLEEP BENEATH THE EARTH; IT IS THE END OF EVERYTHING, EVERYTHING, EVERYTHING.

BRONIA AND JÓZEF CAME TO MARIE AS SOON AS THEY COULD, AS DID PIERRE'S BROTHER JACQUES.

THE FRENCH GOVERNMENT IS OFFERING YOU A PENSION.

I DON'T WANT IT. I'M YOUNG ENOUGH TO EARN MY OWN LIVING AND TO PROVIDE FOR MY CHILDREN.

THE SORBONNE IS ASKING ME TO TAKE OVER PIERRE'S TEACHING DUTIES AND HIS LABORATORY. I DON'T KNOW WHAT TO DO.

YOU WOULD BE THE FIRST WOMAN IN HISTORY TO TEACH AT THE SORBONNE.

PIERRE ALWAYS SAID, WHATEVER HAPPENS, EVEN IF ONE HAS TO GO ON LIKE A BODY WITHOUT A SOUL, ONE MUST WORK ALL THE SAME...PERHAPS I SHOULD TRY. HE ALWAYS WANTED A FIRST-RATE LABORATORY. I CAN TRY TO CREATE ONE IN HIS HONOR.

MARIE WAS TO GIVE HER FIRST PHYSICS LECTURE ON NOVEMBER 5, 1906. HUNDREDS OF PEOPLE CAME TO ATTEND, INCLUDING REPORTERS, PHOTOGRAPHERS, AND MEMBERS OF HIGH SOCIETY.

A WOMAN LECTURING AT THE FAMOUS SORBONNE! WHO WOULD HAVE THOUGHT THAT WOULD EVER HAPPEN?

WHAT DO YOU THINK SHE'S GOING TO SAY? IS SHE GOING TO TALK ABOUT PIERRE CURIE?

DO YOU THINK SHE'S GOING TO CRY? WIDOWED SO YOUNG, IT'S SO VERY SAD.

AND WITH TWO LITTLE CHILDREN TO RAISE ALL ON HER OWN.

HURRAH!

THERE SHE IS!

WHEN ONE CONSIDERS THE PROGRESS THAT HAS BEEN MADE IN PHYSICS IN THE PAST TEN YEARS...

MARIE HAD RESUMED THE SCIENCE LESSON AT THE PRECISE SENTENCE WHERE PIERRE HAD LEFT IT.

LIFE HAD TO GO ON. MARIE MOVED TO SCEAUX. SHE SET UP GYMNASTIC EQUIPMENT FOR THE GIRLS TO EXERCISE ON, AND HIRED A GOVERNESS TO TEACH THEM POLISH. SHE AND OTHER UNIVERSITY FRIENDS SET UP AN EXPERIMENTAL SCHOOL FOR THEIR YOUNG CHILDREN, WHERE THEY WOULD TEACH THEM THEIR SPECIALTIES.

THOUGH SHE KEPT BUSY, MARIE CONTINUED TO BE VERY SAD, WRITING TO HER FRIEND KAZIA:

"...I WANT TO BRING UP MY CHILDREN AS WELL AS POSSIBLE, BUT EVEN THEY CANNOT WAKEN LIFE IN ME."

OH, MY POOR, POOR FRIEND...

MARIE CONTINUED WITH HER SCIENTIFIC WORK. SHE WROTE A TWO-VOLUME SUMMARY OF RADIOACTIVITY, AND FINALLY ISOLATED PURE RADIUM METAL. SHE WORKED TO ACHIEVE HER AND PIERRE'S DREAM OF CREATING A WORLD-CLASS LABORATORY. IN 1909, PLANS WERE BEGUN TO ESTABLISH A RADIUM INSTITUTE IN PARIS, WHERE SHE WOULD SUPERVISE ITS RADIOACTIVITY LAB.

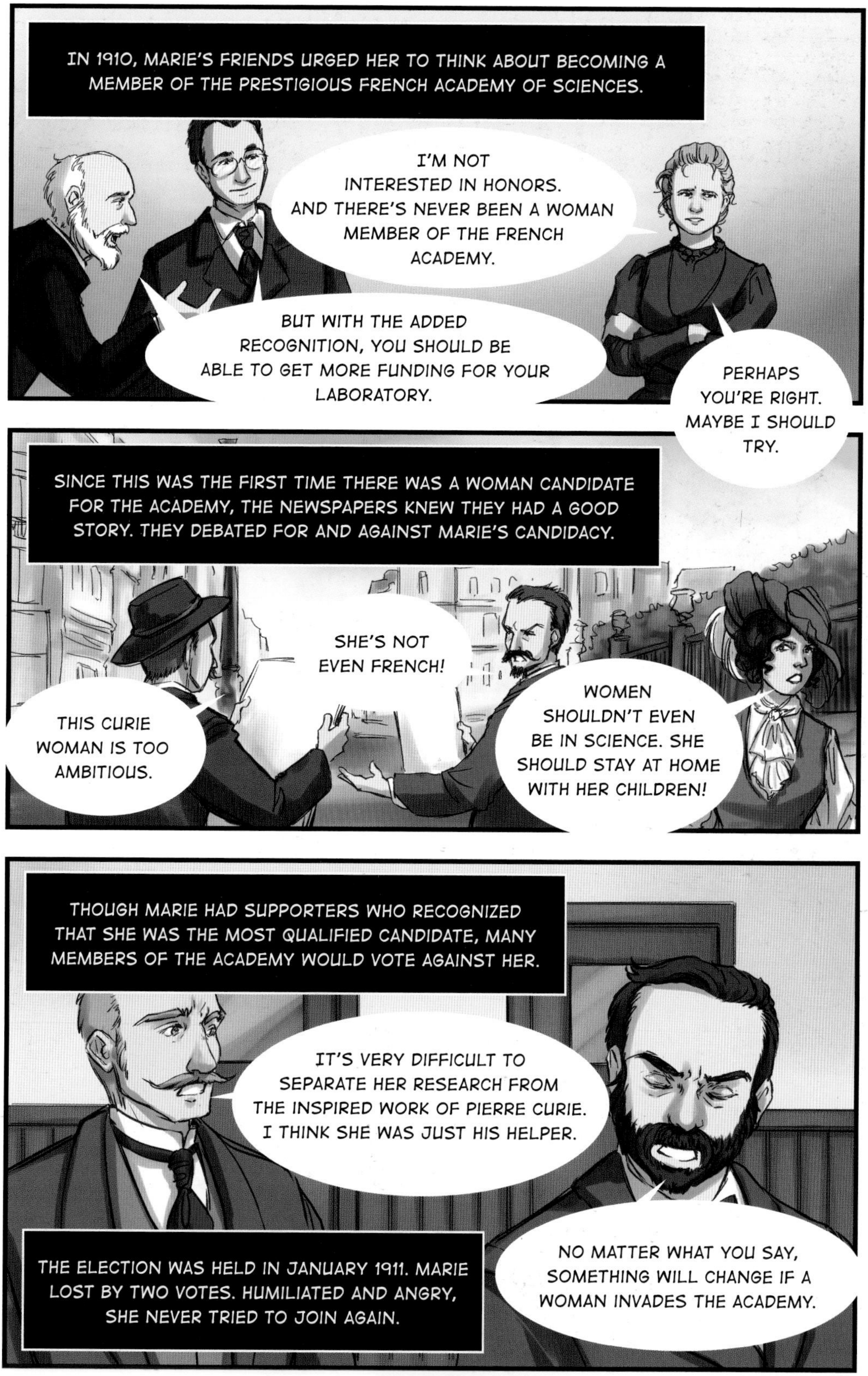
IN 1910, MARIE'S FRIENDS URGED HER TO THINK ABOUT BECOMING A MEMBER OF THE PRESTIGIOUS FRENCH ACADEMY OF SCIENCES.
I'M NOT INTERESTED IN HONORS. AND THERE'S NEVER BEEN A WOMAN MEMBER OF THE FRENCH ACADEMY.
BUT WITH THE ADDED RECOGNITION, YOU SHOULD BE ABLE TO GET MORE FUNDING FOR YOUR LABORATORY.
PERHAPS YOU'RE RIGHT. MAYBE I SHOULD TRY.
SINCE THIS WAS THE FIRST TIME THERE WAS A WOMAN CANDIDATE FOR THE ACADEMY, THE NEWSPAPERS KNEW THEY HAD A GOOD STORY. THEY DEBATED FOR AND AGAINST MARIE'S CANDIDACY.
THIS CURIE WOMAN IS TOO AMBITIOUS.
SHE'S NOT EVEN FRENCH!
WOMEN SHOULDN'T EVEN BE IN SCIENCE. SHE SHOULD STAY AT HOME WITH HER CHILDREN!
THOUGH MARIE HAD SUPPORTERS WHO RECOGNIZED THAT SHE WAS THE MOST QUALIFIED CANDIDATE, MANY MEMBERS OF THE ACADEMY WOULD VOTE AGAINST HER.
IT'S VERY DIFFICULT TO SEPARATE HER RESEARCH FROM THE INSPIRED WORK OF PIERRE CURIE. I THINK SHE WAS JUST HIS HELPER.
NO MATTER WHAT YOU SAY, SOMETHING WILL CHANGE IF A WOMAN INVADES THE ACADEMY.
THE ELECTION WAS HELD IN JANUARY 1911. MARIE LOST BY TWO VOTES. HUMILIATED AND ANGRY, SHE NEVER TRIED TO JOIN AGAIN.

UNFORTUNATELY, MORE BAD PRESS WAS ON THE WAY. IN THE SPRING OF 1910, SOMETHING HAD CHANGED.

WHAT'S HAPPENED TO HER? SHE USUALLY ONLY WEARS BLACK.

I DON'T KNOW.

MARIE HAD FALLEN IN LOVE.

PAUL LANGEVIN WAS A MEMBER OF MARIE'S CIRCLE OF SCIENTIST FRIENDS. FIVE YEARS YOUNGER THAN MARIE, HE HAD BEEN A STUDENT OF PIERRE'S AND WAS A BRILLIANT PHYSICIST AND MATHEMATICIAN.

UNFORTUNATELY, HE WAS ALSO UNHAPPILY MARRIED AND HAD CHILDREN. PAUL AND HIS WIFE ARGUED AND FOUGHT ALL THE TIME.

YOU COULD GET A JOB WITH A PRIVATE COMPANY AND BE MAKING FOUR TIMES THE AMOUNT! YOU HAVE CHILDREN TO SUPPORT! YOU PLACE SCIENCE ABOVE YOUR FAMILY!

MOST OF PAUL'S FRIENDS KNEW OF HIS TROUBLES WITH HIS WIFE.

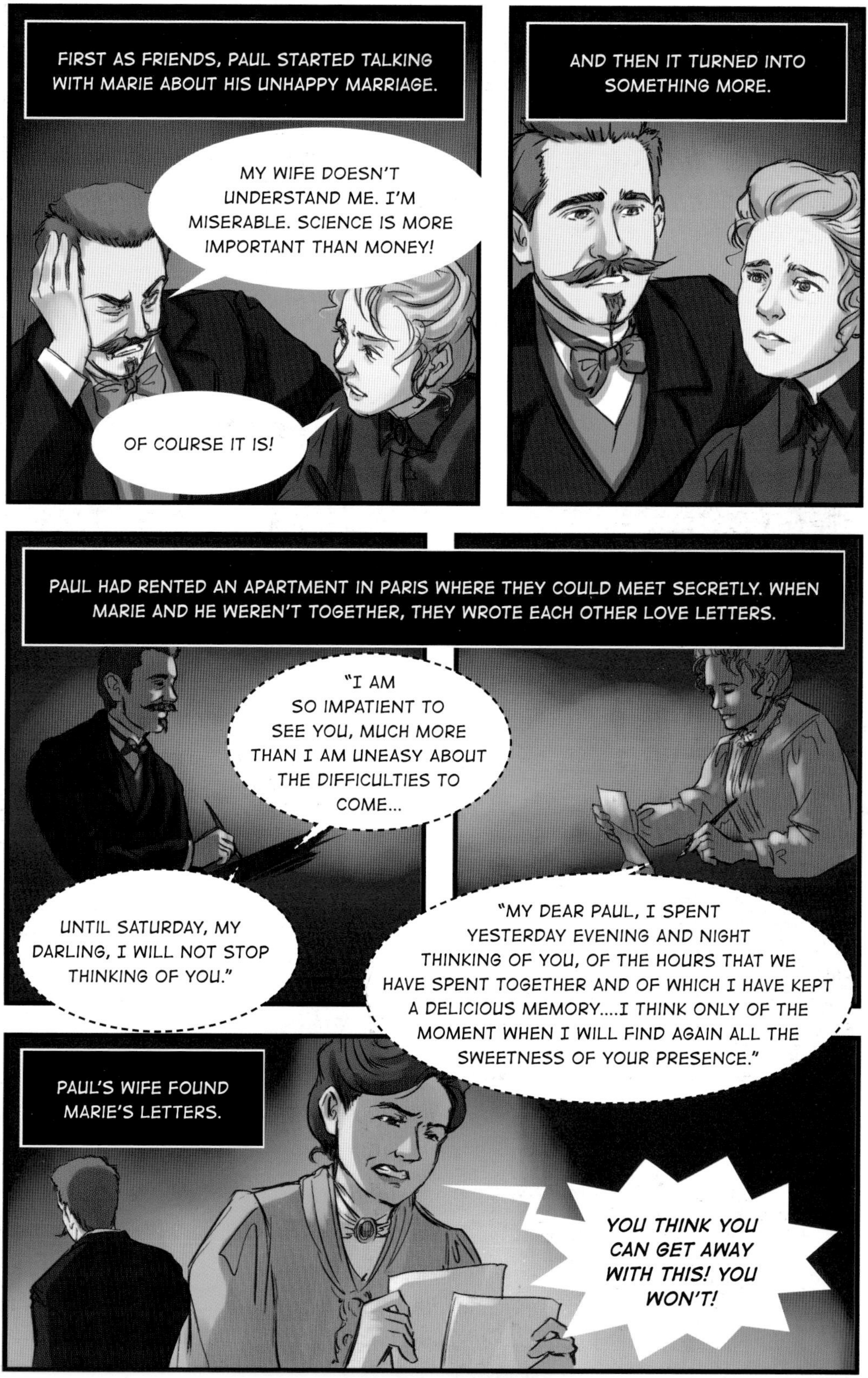
FIRST AS FRIENDS, PAUL STARTED TALKING WITH MARIE ABOUT HIS UNHAPPY MARRIAGE.
MY WIFE DOESN'T UNDERSTAND ME. I'M MISERABLE. SCIENCE IS MORE IMPORTANT THAN MONEY!
OF COURSE IT IS!
AND THEN IT TURNED INTO SOMETHING MORE.
PAUL HAD RENTED AN APARTMENT IN PARIS WHERE THEY COULD MEET SECRETLY. WHEN MARIE AND HE WEREN'T TOGETHER, THEY WROTE EACH OTHER LOVE LETTERS.
"I AM SO IMPATIENT TO SEE YOU, MUCH MORE THAN I AM UNEASY ABOUT THE DIFFICULTIES TO COME...
UNTIL SATURDAY, MY DARLING, I WILL NOT STOP THINKING OF YOU."
"MY DEAR PAUL, I SPENT YESTERDAY EVENING AND NIGHT THINKING OF YOU, OF THE HOURS THAT WE HAVE SPENT TOGETHER AND OF WHICH I HAVE KEPT A DELICIOUS MEMORY....I THINK ONLY OF THE MOMENT WHEN I WILL FIND AGAIN ALL THE SWEETNESS OF YOUR PRESENCE."
PAUL'S WIFE FOUND MARIE'S LETTERS.
YOU THINK YOU CAN GET AWAY WITH THIS! YOU WON'T!

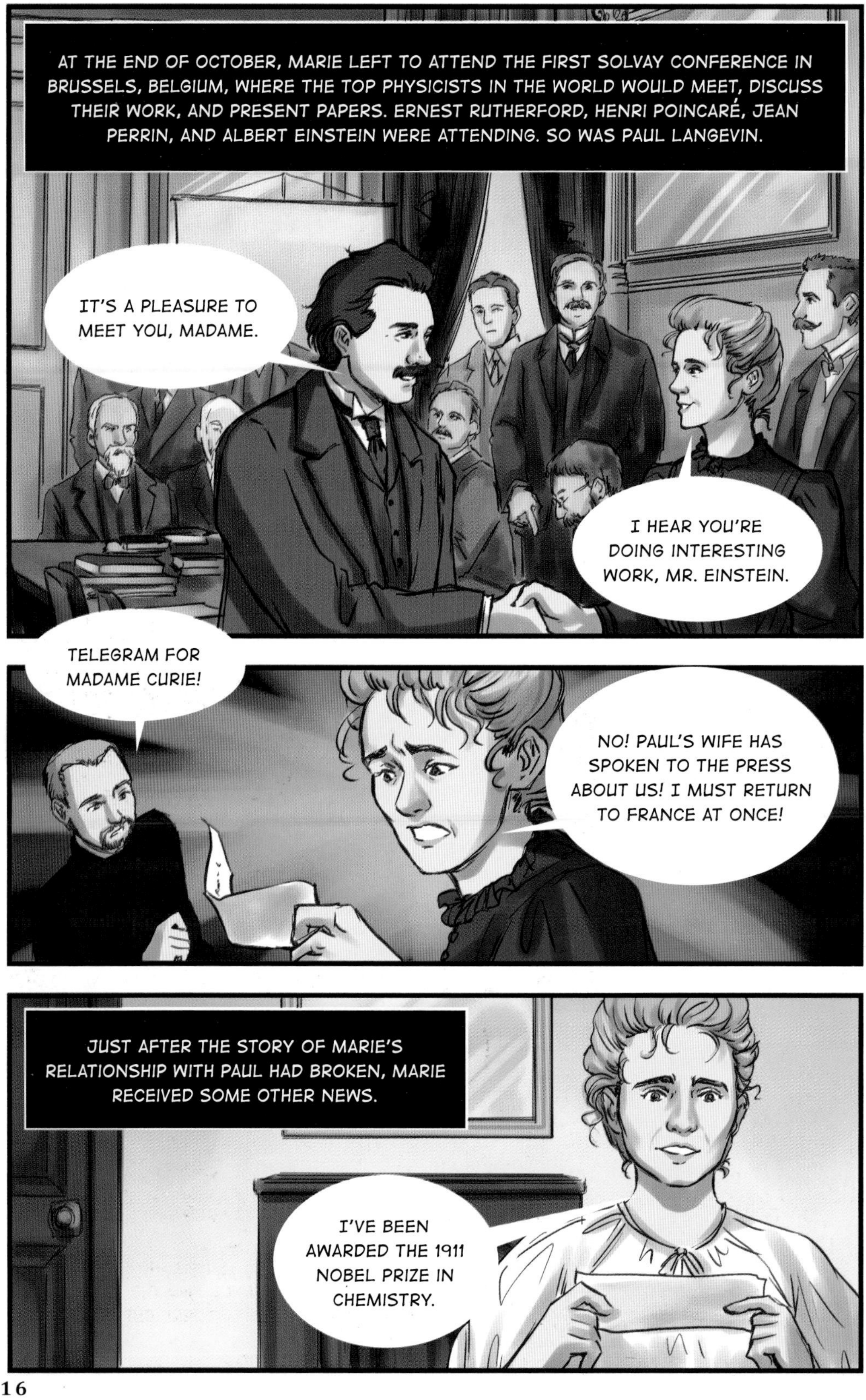
AT THE END OF OCTOBER, MARIE LEFT TO ATTEND THE FIRST SOLVAY CONFERENCE IN BRUSSELS, BELGIUM, WHERE THE TOP PHYSICISTS IN THE WORLD WOULD MEET, DISCUSS THEIR WORK, AND PRESENT PAPERS. ERNEST RUTHERFORD, HENRI POINCARÉ, JEAN PERRIN, AND ALBERT EINSTEIN WERE ATTENDING. SO WAS PAUL LANGEVIN.
IT'S A PLEASURE TO MEET YOU, MADAME.
I HEAR YOU'RE DOING INTERESTING WORK, MR. EINSTEIN.
TELEGRAM FOR MADAME CURIE!
NO! PAUL'S WIFE HAS SPOKEN TO THE PRESS ABOUT US! I MUST RETURN TO FRANCE AT ONCE!
JUST AFTER THE STORY OF MARIE'S RELATIONSHIP WITH PAUL HAD BROKEN, MARIE RECEIVED SOME OTHER NEWS.
I'VE BEEN AWARDED THE 1911 NOBEL PRIZE IN CHEMISTRY.

THE FRENCH NEWSPAPERS IGNORED MARIE'S UNPRECEDENTED SECOND NOBEL PRIZE. THEY WERE MORE INTERESTED IN HER RELATIONSHIP WITH PAUL LANGEVIN. STORIES ATTACKING MARIE RAN FOR WEEKS, MANY FILLED WITH LIES AND HORRIBLE RUMORS.

DID YOU SEE WHAT THIS DIRTY FOREIGN WOMAN HAS DONE? SHE SHOULD GO BACK TO WHEREVER SHE CAME FROM!

ABSOLUTELY DISGUSTING—BREAKING UP A PROPER FRENCH HOME.

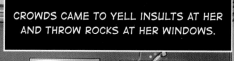

CROWDS CAME TO YELL INSULTS AT HER AND THROW ROCKS AT HER WINDOWS.

DOWN WITH THE FOREIGNER!

HUSBAND-STEALER!

GO BACK TO POLAND!

SOME PROFESSORS AT THE SORBONNE ALSO FELT SHE SHOULD LEAVE FRANCE.

THIS SCANDAL IS TERRIBLE FOR THE UNIVERSITY.

SHE IS DISHONORING FRANCE AND THE NAME OF PIERRE CURIE!

ALBERT EINSTEIN, ANGRY AT HOW MARIE WAS BEING TREATED, WROTE HER A LETTER TO TRY TO CHEER HER UP.

FIVE DUELS WERE FOUGHT IN MARIE'S HONOR, ONE WITH A SWORD. EVEN PAUL LANGEVIN FELT HE HAD TO CHALLENGE A NEWSPAPER EDITOR OVER ONE STORY. REPORTERS WERE THERE TO WITNESS IT.

ONE, TWO, THREE. FIRE!

"IF THE RABBLE CONTINUES TO BE OCCUPIED WITH YOU, SIMPLY STOP READING THAT DRIVEL. LEAVE IT TO THE VIPERS IT WAS FABRICATED FOR."

NEITHER FIRED A SHOT.

I AM NOT AN ASSASSIN.

LOYAL FRIENDS TOOK MARIE AND HER DAUGHTERS IN, WORRIED ABOUT THEIR SAFETY. JÓZEF, BRONIA, AND HELENA CAME TO SUPPORT THEIR SISTER.

COME BACK TO POLAND WITH US. IT'S HORRIBLE HOW THEY'RE TREATING YOU HERE.

MY CHILDREN ARE FRENCH AND MY LIFE IS IN FRANCE NOW. I MUST CONTINUE WITH MY WORK AT THE RADIUM INSTITUTE IF I CAN.

AFTER NEWS OF THE DUEL AND MARIE'S LETTERS WERE PUBLISHED IN THE PRESS, MARIE RECEIVED A LETTER FROM THE NOBEL COMMITTEE ABOUT HER PRIZE.

MARIE, DEFIANT AND ANGRY, WROTE BACK TO SAY THAT SHE WOULD BE ATTENDING.

THEY ARE SAYING THAT I WOULDN'T HAVE BEEN GIVEN THE PRIZE IF THEY KNEW THE RUMORS WERE TRUE.

THEY ARE TELLING ME THAT I SHOULDN'T COME TO THE PRIZE CEREMONY.

THEY WOULD NEVER MAKE THIS KIND OF A REQUEST OF A MAN!

"IN FACT THE PRIZE HAS BEEN AWARDED FOR THE DISCOVERY OF RADIUM AND POLONIUM. I BELIEVE THAT THERE IS NO CONNECTION BETWEEN MY SCIENTIFIC WORK AND THE FACTS OF MY PRIVATE LIFE."

ON DECEMBER 11, 1911, MARIE, ACCOMPANIED BY BRONIA AND IRÈNE, DELIVERED HER NOBEL LECTURE IN SWEDEN. WHILE PAYING TRIBUTE TO PIERRE, SHE MADE VERY CLEAR WHAT HER OWN CONTRIBUTIONS WERE, AND WHAT DISCOVERIES SHE HAD MADE AFTER HIS DEATH.

UPON HER RETURN TO PARIS, SHE WAS RUSHED TO A HOSPITAL. HER HEALTH HAD BROKEN UNDER THE STRAIN.

CHAPTER 11

A WORLD WAR AND LATER LIFE

THROUGHOUT 1912, MARIE WAS TOO ILL AND DEPRESSED TO WORK. HER RELATIONSHIP WITH PAUL LANGEVIN WAS OVER. SHE HAD AN OPERATION ON HER KIDNEYS. HER DAUGHTERS WERE KEPT UNDER THE CARE OF GOVERNESSES AS MARIE TRIED TO GET BETTER.

IN JULY 1912, MARIE VISITED ENGLAND AND STAYED WITH HER FRIEND HERTHA AYRTON, ALSO A SCIENTIST. UNDER HERTHA'S CARE, MARIE GRADUALLY RECOVERED HER HEALTH AFTER HER SURGERY.

YOUR DAUGHTERS WILL BE HERE SOON.

I HAVEN'T SEEN THEM SINCE I'VE BEEN SICK. I'VE MISSED THEM!

MARIE RETURNED TO FRANCE IN OCTOBER. THOUGH STILL NOT WELL, SHE STARTED TAKING UP HER SCIENTIFIC LIFE AGAIN.

I NEED TO FINALIZE THE STANDARD FOR RADIUM THAT WILL BE USED ALL OVER THE WORLD.

AS THE MEMORY OF THE LANGEVIN SCANDAL FADED, SHE STARTED GETTING BACK IN TOUCH WITH FRIENDS. SHE TOOK A HIKING VACATION IN THE ALPS WITH HER DAUGHTERS, JOINING ALBERT EINSTEIN AND HIS SON.

MOST IMPORTANT, THE RADIUM INSTITUTE THAT MARIE DREAMED OF TOOK SHAPE.

I NEED HUGE LAB ROOMS, BIG WINDOWS FOR LIGHT, AND AN ELEVATOR!

I WANT THE TREES PLANTED NOW SO THAT WHEN THE INSTITUTE OPENS THEY'LL BE BIG AND FULL! AND ROSES, TOO!

BUT BEFORE THE INSTITUTE OPENED, WAR BROKE OUT IN JULY 1914. THE GERMANS DECLARED WAR ON FRANCE ON AUGUST 3, AND SOON A MULTITUDE OF COUNTRIES BECAME INVOLVED IN WHAT WAS TO BECOME WORLD WAR I.

EVERYONE IS GONE. ALL MY MALE COLLEAGUES AND STUDENTS HAVE LEFT TO SERVE.

MARIE WANTED TO MELT HER GOLD NOBEL PRIZES FOR THE WAR EFFORT, BUT WAS REFUSED. SHE MOVED HER VALUABLE SUPPLY OF RADIUM FROM PARIS TO A VAULT IN BORDEAUX TO KEEP IT SAFE FROM THE GERMANS.

THERE MUST BE MORE I CAN DO!

X-RAY EQUIPMENT IS SCARCE AND IT COULD BE VERY HELPFUL TO DOCTORS TREATING WOUNDED SOLDIERS.

I CAN ASSEMBLE X-RAY UNITS THAT CAN BE USED AT HOSPITALS.

SHE ASKED LABS AND MANUFACTURERS FOR ANY X-RAY EQUIPMENT THEY HAD, AND ASKED FOR DONATIONS OF CARS AS WELL.

I'VE INVENTED A PORTABLE X-RAY MACHINE THAT COULD BE POWERED BY A CAR MOTOR IF NECESSARY.

BRILLIANT! WE COULD DO X-RAYS ON THE BATTLEFIELD WHERE THEY'RE NEEDED MOST!

MARIE EQUIPPED 20 CARS AS WELL AS ABOUT 200 FIXED INSTALLATIONS WITH X-RAY EQUIPMENT. SHE SET UP A RADIOLOGY COURSE AND TRAINED 150 WOMEN TO USE THE EQUIPMENT.

MARIE TAUGHT HERSELF TO DRIVE AND TO FIX CARS AS WELL. HER MOBILE X-RAY CARS SOON STARTED TO BE CALLED "LITTLE CURIES."

ON SEVERAL TRIPS TO HELP THE WOUNDED, MARIE WAS HELPED BY IRÈNE, NOW 17. IT'S SAID THAT OVER A MILLION SOLDIERS WERE EXAMINED USING MARIE'S EQUIPMENT.

IT WON'T HURT. IT'S JUST LIKE TAKING A PHOTOGRAPH.

IRÈNE, PLEASE HELP HIM UP.

WHEN PEACE WAS DECLARED IN 1918, MARIE REJOICED.

AND WITH THE PEACE TREATY, POLAND IS NOW A FREE COUNTRY AGAIN, AFTER 123 LONG YEARS!

123

AFTER THE WAR, MARIE'S RADIUM INSTITUTE BECAME A WORLD CENTER FOR THE STUDY OF RADIOACTIVITY.

RADIUM IS ONE OF THE WORLD'S MOST EXPENSIVE SUBSTANCES, AND THE INSTITUTE HAS ONLY ONE GRAM. WE NEED MORE MONEY AND MORE RADIUM FOR OUR RESEARCH.

MARIE TOURED THE U.S. AND WAS GREETED BY HUGE CROWDS. SHE RECEIVED MANY HONORS. AMONG THEM WAS A GRAM OF RADIUM...

...PRESENTED TO HER BY PRESIDENT WARREN HARDING. A RESEARCH-FUNDING DRIVE AMONG WOMEN HAD RAISED THE MONEY TO BUY IT.

MARIE ALSO HELPED ESTABLISH A SECOND RADIUM INSTITUTE IN WARSAW. IT OFFICIALLY OPENED IN 1932 WITH BRONIA AS ITS FIRST DIRECTOR.

PEOPLE EVENTUALLY STARTED REALIZING THE DANGER OF WORKING WITH RADIOACTIVE MATERIALS.

MY EYES ARE VERY WEAK NOW...AND MY HANDS ARE SO SCARRED.

AS SHE GREW OLDER AND SICKER, MARIE WAS HELPED BY HER DAUGHTERS. IRÈNE BECAME A SCIENTIST WORKING ALONGSIDE HER MOTHER AND LATER WON A NOBEL PRIZE HERSELF.

ÈVE BECAME A JOURNALIST AND WROTE HER MOTHER'S FIRST BIOGRAPHY.

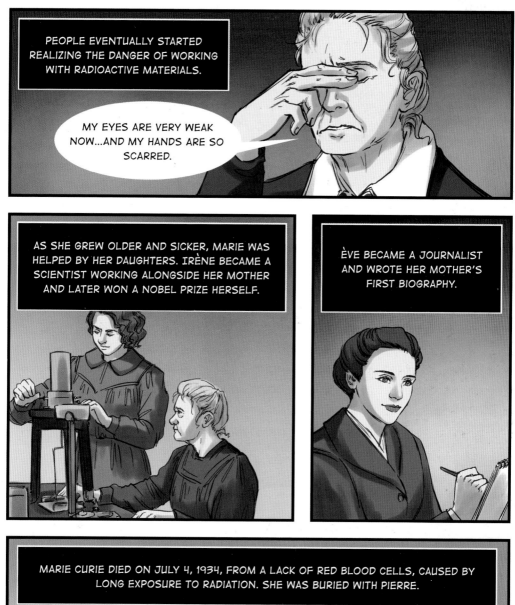

MARIE CURIE DIED ON JULY 4, 1934, FROM A LACK OF RED BLOOD CELLS, CAUSED BY LONG EXPOSURE TO RADIATION. SHE WAS BURIED WITH PIERRE.

BRONIA AND JÓZEF CAME FROM WARSAW, EACH SCATTERING A HANDFUL OF POLISH SOIL OVER HER COFFIN.

125

MARIE'S ACCOMPLISHMENTS ENCOURAGED WOMEN AROUND THE WORLD TO BECOME SCIENTISTS. HER DETERMINATION AGAINST ALL OBSTACLES WAS A SHINING EXAMPLE OF WHAT A PERSON COULD ACCOMPLISH IF HE OR SHE WERE WILLING TO WORK HARD.

EVEN TODAY, SHE REMAINS THE MOST FAMOUS WOMAN IN SCIENCE, THE FIRST PERSON EVER TO WIN TWO NOBEL PRIZES. BUILDINGS AND SCHOOLS ARE NAMED FOR HER, MUSEUMS ARE DEVOTED TO HER LIFE, AND HER IMAGE HAS BEEN USED ON STAMPS, COINS, AND PAPER MONEY. ON THE FAR SIDE OF THE MOON ARE THE CURIE AND SKŁODOWSKA CRATERS.

IN 1944, SCIENTISTS AT THE UNIVERSITY OF CALIFORNIA, BERKELEY, DISCOVERED AN ELEMENT THAT THEY NAMED CURIUM IN HER AND PIERRE'S HONOR.

MARIE, LIKE PIERRE, FEARED THAT RADIOACTIVE MATERIALS MIGHT BE TURNED INTO WEAPONS. UNFORTUNATELY, THEY WERE RIGHT. AMERICAN SCIENTISTS USED URANIUM TO CREATE ATOMIC BOMBS IN 1945 THAT WERE DROPPED ON JAPAN AT THE END OF WORLD WAR II, KILLING HUNDREDS OF THOUSANDS OF PEOPLE.

AT THE SAME TIME, RADIATION ALSO HAS MANY BENEFITS. IT'S USED TO TREAT CANCER, PRODUCE ELECTRICITY, KILL ORGANISMS THAT SPOIL FOOD, ESTIMATE THE AGE OF FOSSILS, AND MORE. MARIE'S WORK CHANGED SCIENTISTS' UNDERSTANDING OF THE ATOM, ONCE UNIVERSALLY THOUGHT TO BE A CONSTANT, STABLE, UNCHANGING BLOCK OF MATTER.

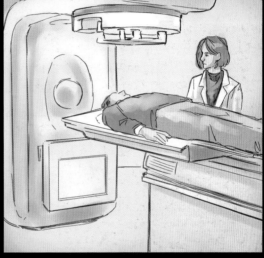

IN 1995, PIERRE AND MARIE'S REMAINS WERE MOVED TO THE PANTHEON, A BUILDING IN PARIS WHERE FRANCE'S MOST IMPORTANT PEOPLE ARE BURIED. AT LONG LAST, MARIE WAS AWARDED THE HIGHEST HONOR THAT FRANCE COULD BESTOW.

ACKNOWLEDGMENTS

Agnieszka Biskup: Graphic novels, by their nature, have limited text. You have to choose your words carefully and can't always include everything you'd like. Similarly, I can't acknowledge all the people who helped and supported me during my writing. But I do especially want to thank my sister Teresa, a librarian, for providing books and materials for my research, as well as my mother Helena, a former Polish schoolteacher, for looking over the first draft and providing comments. (Yes, I know it should be *mazurek*, not *mazurka*.) Thank you both!

Sonia Leong: Marie Curie was an amazing person. Her struggles with depression, balancing her work with her personal life, and her fight to be recognized for her achievements really resonated with me, so it was such an honor to be able to illustrate her story. Huge thanks to my editor Anna for her encouragement and support especially during difficult times, and much love to my husband Matthew for infinite tea, foot rubs, and help in managing the household when I was crunching deadlines!